DORIT'S GARDEN

Memoirs of the Holocaust

Never forget!
6/5/24

Angie Sultan Osers

First Paperback Edition March 2023

Copyright ©2023 Angie Sultan Osers

All rights reserved

Photographs and Images collected by Harry & Dorit during their lives and preserved over the years by the Osers Family.

Photograph of KAMARAD newspaper, no. 1, cover Courtesy of Beit Theresienstadt, Kibbutz Givat Hayim-Ihud, Israel.

Photograph of Harry Osers Meal Portion Serving Cup Courtesy of Jose Daniel Urdaneta Ballesteros

Cover art, book design, & edited by Judith Osers Muller

Dedication

This memoir is dedicated to all the Jews that were brutally murdered by the Nazis; especially to those whose stories will never be heard.

To my grandparents, who were immersed in the worst of human conditions and never gave up.

To my parents and uncles who are committed to Holocaust education and remembrance, so it's never denied, ignored, or forgotten.

And to my kids. I wrote this for you, and your future generations.

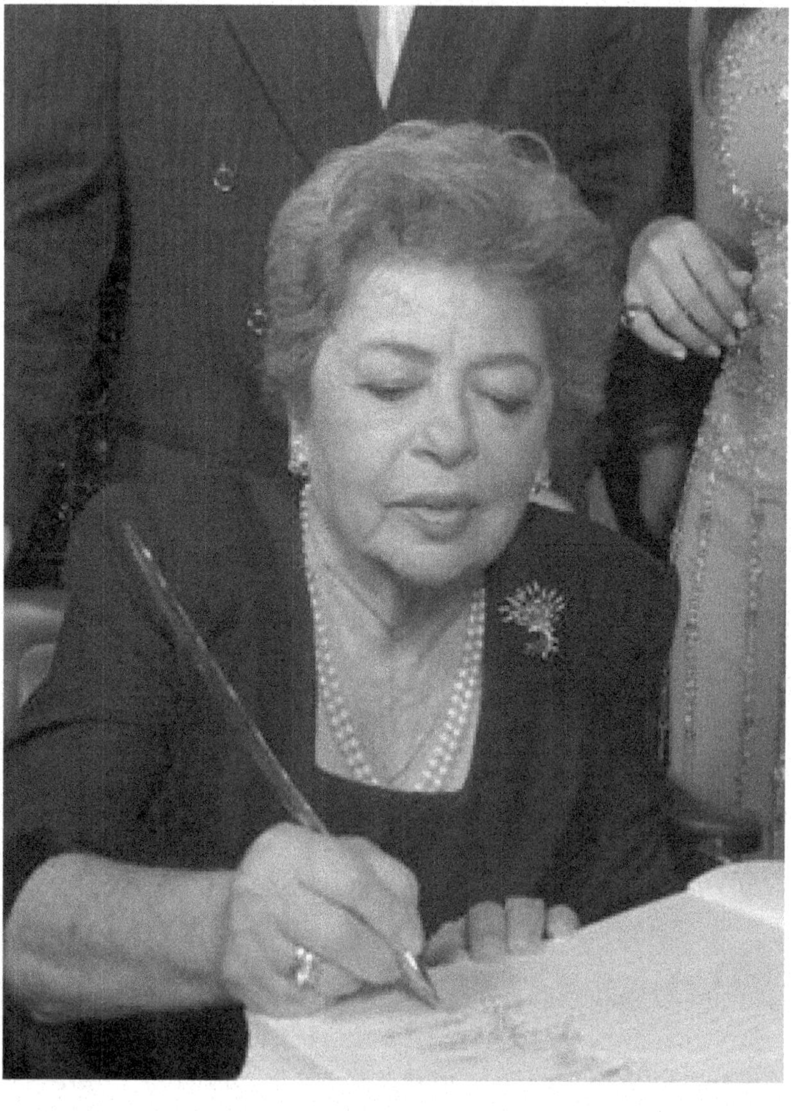

Dorit Weiss, 1935-2006

"At the beginning, when we left the concentration camps, we didn't have the need to say what happened to us; we had to organize our lives, work, and start a family.

But now that we are getting older and we have more free time, now is the time to tell what happened to us, maybe with a little less pain."

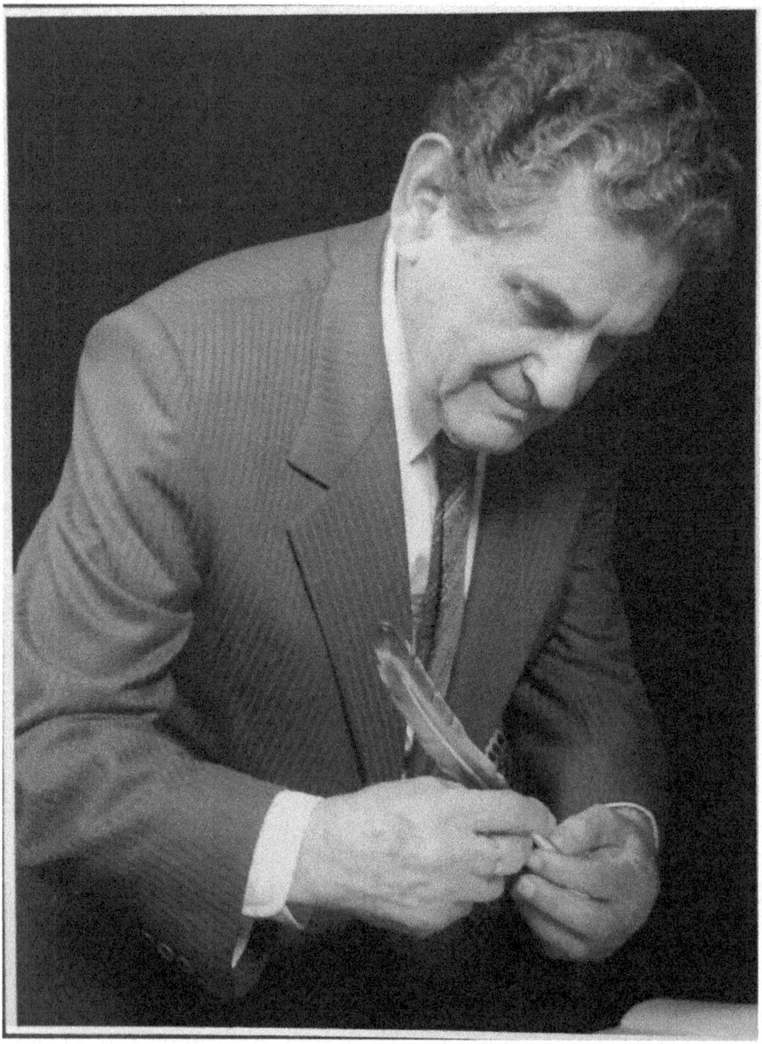

Harry Osers, 1929-2013

"What I had to go through in my youth was an awful experience that made me a really strong and emotionally tough person. I was always able and willing to recount what happened to me before, during and after the holocaust, with all the details I could remember, to anyone that wanted to hear my story.

But it was just now, when I first read Angie's book about me and my wife Dorit's life, written in her own words, that I shed my first tear because of what happened to us during the War."

Contents

DORIT'S GARDEN 1
Dedication 3
Dorit Weiss, 1935-2006 5
Harry Osers, 1929-2013 7
Contents 8
    HARRY: The good old days 9
    DORIT: Lucky me 25
    HARRY: Off we go, a trip to hell 33
    DORIT: Scary moments 46
    HARRY: Best of the worst. 50
    DORIT: My life in the camp 69
    HARRY: Saved by "The Angel of Death" 76
    DORIT: The war garden 89
    HARRY: The odyssey 92
    DORIT: The cruel reality 104
    HARRY: My liberation 110
    DORIT: The end of the war 118
    HARRY: Back to Prague and beyond 124
    DORIT: More changes 135
    HARRY: Together in Venezuela 142
Epilogue 144
Acknowledgment 148

I

HARRY: The good old days

One fall afternoon in November of 1942, four months after my Bar mitzvah, my family received the tremendously feared piece of paper: The letter from the *Judenrat* informing us that we were selected to be included in the next transportation train denoted with the letters "Cc".

We were so afraid not to follow the order, even when we didn't know exactly where they were taking us, but we had the feeling it wasn't going to be good. Most likely it would be Theresienstadt. Most Jews in this situation were doubting what to do, they were scared, mortified, worried about the uncertain future ahead. Only a lucky few were able to escape.

We lived in Prague. My beloved city, where I was born and raised. Also known as the Heart of Europe, not only because of its geographic location, but also its cultural richness. City of Gothic and Baroque stone architecture, of castles and arched bridges, of pointy towers that stick out like needles in the horizon. Named today a World Heritage site by UNESCO.

I really can't complain about my youth. My family had a good social and financial status. We owned a pretty apartment in a very nice, new neighborhood in the city. We were one of the first families in the area that owned a refrigerator. We were able to receive a top-notch education filled with sports and different activities. During vacation time we were able to travel through Europe, which was unusual for Czech citizens. We went to France, Monaco, Belgium, and Austria among other wonderful places. Went skiing in the winter, hiking in the summer, but in my opinion none of these were as good as my good old Prague. As you can imagine by now, we were a happy little family: My dad, my mom, my sister, and myself.

MY MOM, MY SISTER AND ME.

My name is Harry Osers, I was born on May 1st, 1929. My father Rodolfo worked as the director of a food trading company, importing, and selling food, which was the reason why we never ever had a shortage of food at home, at least until then. My mom Maria was a stay-at-home mom, always taking care of my dad, my older sister Sonia, and me. She was in charge of the house chores along with our housekeeper Anna, who lived in the apartment with us.

My elementary school was really close to my house, so we used to walk every day to it. I was a very good student. I liked all the classes except one: Music. I definitely can't sing! We were approximately forty students, of which two and a half were Jewish; the half meant that his dad was Jewish, but his mom wasn't. But we were all friends; there wasn't any discrimination between us.

I will never forget my elementary teacher who taught me for five years straight, Mr. Karel Veselý (very appropriately his last name means Happy in Czech). He was a wonderful person, teacher, and role model. I can thank him for the foundation of my education, and partly for the spiritual strength that I dare to say I have. I still have engraved in my mind the words of advice that he constantly repeated: "Be morally correct and always have the truth as your flag".

PROF KAREL VESELY 1938-39

Aside from spending time studying for school, I was a member of the Jewish swimming club called Hagibor (It means the strong one). I immensely enjoyed going to practice and competitions. We used to win a lot of tournaments and medals in water polo. We were the number one team in the entire country and all the other clubs were always trying to beat us.

Jewish people living in Prague felt like any other Czech citizen, there weren't any differences between us and the non-Jewish, and we never thought that could or would change. There were many synagogues in the city; my family belonged to one named Pinkas, the second oldest synagogue in Prague. Like most of the Czech Jews, we only attended for the high holidays every year.

I remember that my non-Jewish friends loved visiting the synagogue because they knew they handed out candy to children in some festivities. They would try to pass as Jewish kids, but it was very easy to recognize them, since contrary to Jewish tradition, they would take off their hat when they entered the building instead of putting one on (the kippah). We had religion classes once a week where we learned about the history written in the Old Testament and about the festivities and other traditions.

ME AND MY DAD.

I will make a small parenthesis to give you some context before continuing with my story.

The plan for the global destruction and elimination of the Jewish people in Europe was developed by the Nazis long before its execution and was implemented very methodically in all German occupied territories.

In September of 1935, the Nazi Party decreed the Nuremberg Laws, which deprived Jews of German citizenship and civil rights. It also prohibited racially mixed marriages or sexual relations between "Aryan" and "non-Aryan" to protect and guarantee the purity of the German "Aryan" race, blood, and lineage. To help achieve their goal, they had to legally classify a Jew as any person whose lineage included a Jewish relative in any of their previous three generations. Then they defined two very distinctive groups: The Aryan or pure Germanic Nordics (believed to be a superior Master race), and the non-Aryans which included Jews, gypsies, and people of color.

To help with the annihilation logistics, the Germans formed the so-called Judenrats —Jewish councils- in every occupied city so that they could organize, administer and supervise all Jewish matters. Mostly handling the preparation and implementation of all the laws and German decrees. When the Germans started sending lists of people that needed to be deported, the Judenrat was in charge of finding those people and giving them notice, informing them where they needed to go, as well as how and when to do so. After everyone was relocated, they sent the information back to the Gestapo – Secret state- so they had a record of every Non-Aryan in each city.

To minimize the resistance from the non-Aryan, the Germans planned a slow, gradual, and systematic denigration of their honor and human dignity by constantly dictating new public decrees, which commanded or prohibited them from certain activities with the death penalty as the consequence for disobedience.

In March of 1939, the Germans occupied my country, Czechoslovakia, and slowly we started feeling all the discrimination against us.

One day, somebody knocked on our door. My mom opened it and a German officer came inside. He told us we had to surrender all our radios and music devices, as well as all our jewelry, including wedding rings, fur clothing items, sports equipment like skis and bikes; pretty much everything that was valuable or considered a luxury. This was a very sad day for our family. Imagine giving away all the things you earned with hard work, all the things that made you happy? Most of these items we had to turn in right away, but luckily, we were able to hide and save a few valuable things. We later handed them over to my teacher Mr. Vesely, who risked his own life by helping us and kept our possessions during the war. He returned everything when we came back home after the war was over.

In the beginning, my parents tried really hard to hide what was going on, they didn't want us to see and feel all the unfairness and abuses from the Germans. It took my sister and I a while to understand all the bad things that were happening. We were still going to school and our lives continued. My parents, suspecting what was coming, started doing the necessary paperwork to emigrate to The United States of America. What they didn't contemplate was how fast everything would happen. I guess they didn't do it fast or early enough.

After the officer visited our house, the situation worsened almost every day. We were prohibited from leaving our house after eight o'clock, and we couldn't use any public transportation. Slowly we couldn't even enter public places like parks, museums, libraries, restaurants, theaters, stores, or even public restrooms. All these establishments had a sign that read:

"Juden Eintritt Verboten"

"Jews Entry Prohibited"

After that, they also prohibited the entrance and participation of Jews in sport complexes and public schools, from elementary to colleges. When I finished elementary school at the age of twelve, I took, and passed, the test to enter middle school but I wasn't allowed to register. At the same time, they prohibited us from swimming and competing in any sporting event. That year, finally a non-Jewish swimming club won the national competition taking the 1st place that we always had. That day I was not only sad and upset, but I was also mad. I was finally feeling in my own experience what it was to be discriminated against because of my religion. I understood how unfair it was, and the worst part was I couldn't do anything about it. I couldn't hide those feelings anymore, neither could my parents.

One night after we were done with dinner, I saw my mom sewing yellow fabric stars onto our coats and sweaters. They were all exactly the same, with ten centimeters in diameter and the word JUDE written in black in the middle. The *Judenrat* had distributed these stars during the day, providing two per person. That same night my mom sat in our room and explained to us:

"Dearest children, from now on, all of us must always wear these stars visible when we are outside in the streets. We must carry it on our left side, near our hearts; it's our public identification as Jews".

When we went outside the following day, everybody knew who was and who wasn't a Jew. I carried my star with pride and a little fear at the same time. Sometimes my dad would get a messenger bag and wear it in a way that it would "cover" the star when he went to get food at his friend Mr. Joseph Hruska's house. He was the director of a very big and important industrial bakery in Prague where most of the flour goods for the city were baked.

May 1942 (Only 10 survived)

Since we didn't have many distractions and things to do at home, my parents decided to get us a little puppy. One day my dad came to the house with a little white and brown fox terrier dog who we called Dáshenka, after one of our favorite books "Dáshenka, or the Life of a Puppy" by Karel Čapek, one of the best known and most popular Czech books. We loved her and played so much with her. It really brought a lot of happiness to our house.

One day, we saw through our window a couple of kids playing in the park with a dog. Immediately we started thinking, if Dáshenka runs away and enters the park we wouldn't be able to go after her and get her. The same afternoon we sat down with her and explained to her that she was a Jewish dog, and as one, she wasn't allowed to go to the park or any of the public places we couldn't go. Then we invented a song about how dangerous it was for a Jewish dog to run away to places like the park because she could get lost or punished and never come back to us. We felt really bad and sorry for the doggy, locked in the house all day every day. She must have been feeling the same way because she passed away a couple of months later.

We lived very comfortably in our house until 1941, when we heard a German liked our apartment and decided he wanted it for himself.

They made us move to a building in the Old Prague quarter known as "The Ghetto". The move was pretty quick, my mom told us to grab our most valuable and important belongings (whatever we had left) and we departed. Lots of furniture and memories were left behind.

We were assigned a small apartment that we had to share with two other families. Each family had one bedroom. We all shared the kitchen and one bathroom. The difference between this Ghetto and the ones in Poland, was that this one wasn't fenced and in the streets, you could see both Jewish and non-Jewish people walking.

Because of all the restrictions and prohibitions for Jewish people in all aspects of society, my dad lost his job, so he decided he could spend some time helping the *Judenrat*. Since Jewish kids couldn't go to school, the Jewish sport club was teaching the kids to play baseball, among other things, in case (hoping) someday we would go to America.

All those days in the Ghetto there was barely anything we could do. So, I spent a lot of my time learning and playing chess. I became really good at it, and it served me well since it played an important role later in my life as a concentration camp inmate.

In October of 1941, the Germans made a prohibition to celebrate or do any religious services in synagogues. These buildings were later used as storage centers for furniture and belongings of relocated or deported Jews. Despite all this, in mid-1942 I was able to celebrate my Bar-mitzvah. It was a very small and simple act but very meaningful. My family just gathered in a room that we transformed into looking like a synagogue, a rabbi came, and we prayed. There wasn't a big banquet or a dancing reception, but my family was so proud of me, and I felt fulfilled.

The emotion and content didn't last long. Only a couple of months later, we received The Letter: We were all to be deported to camps.

II
DORIT: Lucky me

I don't remember the place where I was born, but after the war was over, I went to Czechoslovakia with my family and I went back to visit it. I don't remember much about those pre-war days, as I was really little, but I know I was born in Brno, Cz. on June 10th, 1935.

I can tell you my dad, Pablo Weiss, was an electrical engineer and my mom, Susana Schlesinger de Weiss, worked in an electric cable factory. That's where they met.

I was told we lived a very comfortable, nice life. I even had my own nanny called Hansie. We had a big extended family of about twenty-five relatives including my aunts, uncles, and cousins. Everybody got along very well. I live in our house with my parents, our housekeeper, and our nanny. My name is Dorit Weiss.

1 Willi Weiss (21)
2 Frantisek P (16+19)
3 Rudi Weiss
4 Fritz Weiss (21)
5 Oskar Weiss (21)
6 Ludvik Prager (16)
7 Hans Pollak (25+13)
8 Pavel Weiss
9 Ernst Weiss (21)
10 Carl Weiss (21)
11 Richard P (23)
12 Arthur P. (23)
13 Ludwig Pollak H25
14 Ludwik Weiss H21
15 Otto Weiss
16 Ludvik Prager (23)
17 Robert P (23)
18 Lilly Pollack (25+13)
19 Anna P W16
20 Ida Weiss (23)
21 Rosa Weiss (23)
22 Sussana P (12+26)
23 Teresa P Wignaz Prager
24 George (12+26)

WEISS - PRAGER FAMILY. 1936

(18,4,22,8) SOLE SURVIVORS

I was a beautiful blonde girl that looked like a living porcelain doll, or at least that's what I was told. Hansie always had me dressed in cute expensive dresses and beautiful hairdos. One day walking on the street, we ran into a famous town photographer, and he asked us if he could take a few pictures of me, to which we agreed. A few days later, we were surprised to see a life size picture of me in his shop window.

I was also very friendly, and I liked the way men looked in their uniforms or long white robes, so every time I saw a police officer or a doctor or… a baker, I would smile and flirt with them.

My dad and me.

Back home we only celebrated major Jewish holidays. My parents registered me in a very exclusive private school, but unfortunately, I was only able to attend for a month because the Germans made a law that prohibited Jewish kids from going to school. I remember part of my uniform was an apron that had my name embroidered on it.

Right after that, other restrictions followed. We had to surrender our jewelry, skis, radios, and other items. We couldn't use the trolley, and we couldn't walk on the walkways. I don't know how parents back then explained and enforced that to five-year-old Jewish kids. Maybe their fear was so tremendous that we felt it and somehow all obeyed. I remember my parents always told me to stay calm and quiet, trying to disappear from the eyes of the "*Schutzstaffel*" or SS Nazi guards. I had to be so insignificant that I could go unnoticed.

In front of our home, there was a pretty house with a beautiful garden filled with flowers of all sizes and colors. I loved it. One day, we were walking by, and I picked a few of their flowers… big mistake. The house belonged to an SS officer, and he saw me picking the flowers. He immediately came to my house and told my dad that he could send us to a concentration camp right then. My dad begged him not to, saying we had always been good neighbors and we would keep it that way. Miraculously the officer didn't report us.

As you can imagine, I was in big trouble. My dad was furious and punished me for a long time. I had to learn my lesson, not to pick flowers from other people's gardens, but I don't think the lesson stuck.

I always went shopping with my mom, well, we pretty much did everything together. She used to give me a little handbag where she put the butter she bought. She thought that since I was just a kid I wouldn't be searched. Then she told me:

> "Doritku, always walk a few steps in front or behind me, if you see that someone, especially if a police officer stops me, you ignore me and just keep walking as if you don't know me. Go home and don't look back."

At some point they made it mandatory for us to wear yellow David Stars attached to our clothes. I liked that. But I wasn't as afraid as my parents. Every time someone knocked at our door, they trembled thinking they would send us away.

One day, we got a letter from the post office saying my dad had a package that he needed to pick up. My mom decided to go instead and when she got there the Gestapo was waiting to take her for interrogation. The package was a radio. Apparently, someone sent it to my dad so he, an electrical engineer, would fix it; but it took three days of interrogations for the Gestapo to figure it out. Fortunately, the radio wasn't even working, and they let my mom go.

After that episode, we got displaced from our house to an area of the city with all the other Jews. At the beginning people tried to get together with family or friends so we went to one of my aunt's houses for a while. We were living in her attic. One time my dad was able to find a duck and my mom offered to cook it for us with my aunt, with the condition that we went walking outside making sure the smell wouldn't reach any officer who could come in and report us.

A few weeks later, they evacuated all of us from my aunt's house and made us go to three different places. Eventually, they relocated us to an apartment we had to share with three other families. It wasn't much fun there. Adults were living in fear and really nervous all the time, so the kids had to always be on their best behavior. But for me it wasn't that bad at all. Being an only child, I finally had other kids to play with and talk to. One of the families had a little dog called Gafik, I don't know what breed he was, it was little and all black, and sometimes it ran so fast he would flip over. It became my favorite form of entertainment!

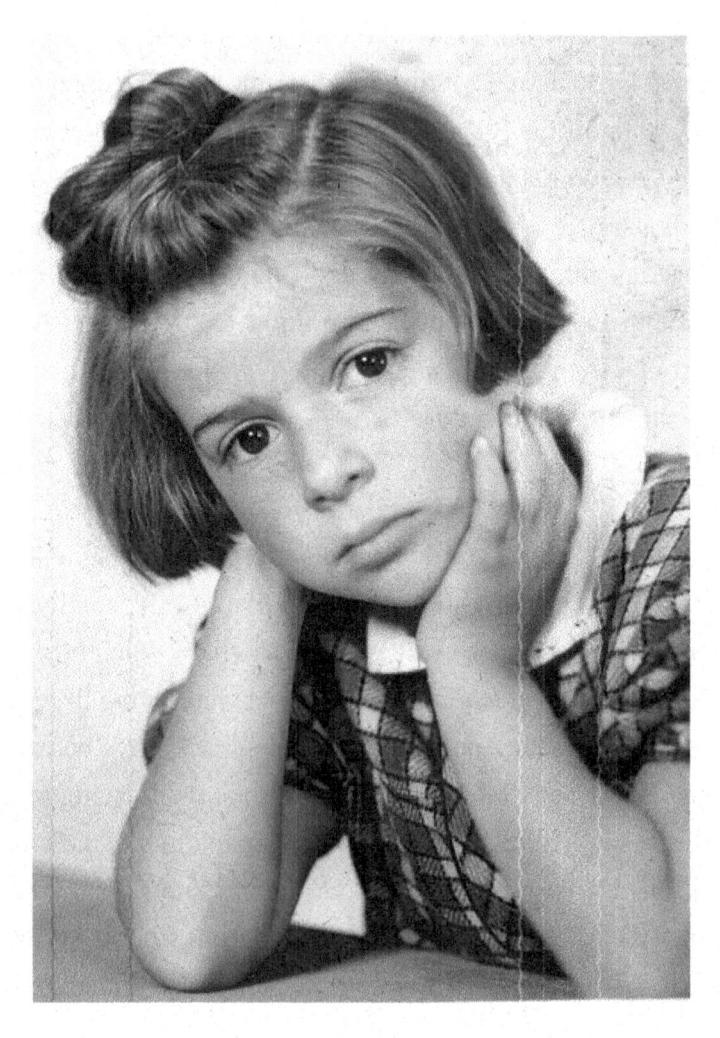

DORIT 1938-1939 BRNO CZECHOSLOVAKIA

III
HARRY: Off we go, a trip to hell

They gathered us at the *Veletrzní Palác,* the city's convention center, where they were sending everyone who was being deported from Prague. There we had to give up our apartment keys and they made us sign a document saying we were moving "voluntarily". After that we each received a paper with a number, mine was Cc476, referencing the transportation train number and passenger number. We remained in that place for three days, awaiting our destiny.

We slept tightly in numeric order on the cold floor and occasionally got some food portions. My dad told us:

"Please eat EVERYTHING you are given, doesn't matter what it is or if you like it or not. I'm afraid food will be very limited, scarce, and sparse for us from now on."

On the third day, they walked us to the train station. All of us, young, old, kids and adults went dragging our few bags and our hopes. Today, there is a new hotel in that convention center and a plaque in memoriam of all who were deported from there to the camps.

Our train was a passenger one, but it had all the windows sealed so they couldn't be opened. The trip was short, about two or three hours and we realized we were going north, which made many people happy including my dad since it was known that things "to the East", in the Polish territories, were much worse. Some acquaintances who were previously deported managed to write letters warning us about Polish concentration camps, like Lodz, Treblinka and Majdanek to name a few.

They took us to a little town named Bohusovice, where we were unloaded from the wagons because the train tracks weren't ready, so they made us walk in groups of five all the way to Theresienstadt. We didn't have a clue of what that was.

We got to Theresienstadt at night, we could only see a few lights and smoke coming out from some chimneys. The first thing we did when we got there was go to the *"Slojska"* where we had to undress completely to go take a shower while they would search through our clothes for valuables. My mom had sewn some money and jewelry in the lining of some coats that they didn't find, and we were able to take that with us. I think one ring even made it back with her to Prague after the war. After the shower they gave us some dinner and sent us to our barracks to sleep.

Theresienstadt, also known as Terezin, was a concentration camp, with all its components: each person became a number; you got your premade portion of food; and men, women and kids slept separately in their barracks. It was pretty much a place to bring people, organize them and send them to death camps. Terezin also was called a ghetto since only Jewish people were sent there, and it was run by the *Judenrat*. We didn't have any mass murders or gas chambers.

Thank God we didn't have much direct contact with the Germans there. There were only about twenty of them guarding the entire camp; we just saw them from far away. Under their command there were Czech officers, and under them the *Judenalteste* – Jewish manager. They also organized a Jewish police unit with the first group of people that were sent there. They were so good at their job and well prepared, that soon after, they were all sent to Auschwitz fearing they could plan a coup.

At the ghetto, it was totally off limits to have cigarettes, lighters, photo cameras, money, write letters or have any other kind of communication with the outside world. If someone was found with any of these, the prisoner would be hung.

The day after our arrival, they started doing all the paperwork for sleeping arrangements and work assignments. Men to one side of the camp, women to the other, and kids separately. For the first couple of days, I was lucky enough to be in the same barracks as my dad, named *Sudeten Kaserne*; they were one of the newest and best ones. The barrack consisted primarily of strong men that were capable of working. Roughly a week after being there, I was moved to another barrack with other teenage boys between twelve and fifteen years old. It was called the *Heim* Q609 barrack.

My mom and sister were together in a barrack named *Hamburger Kaserne*. We saw each other once a week.

Kids at Terezin had certain privileges that didn't exist in any other camp. The camp managers thought it was important to keep educating us, so at the *Heim* they tried to teach us some classes equivalent to the ones we would see at a school, but it was a little complicated since there were kids in at least four different grade levels. We also tried doing other activities to entertain ourselves like sing songs (everyone except me), play chess and practice different ball games, including soccer.

It was in this *Heim* that I met my dear friend Mísa Kraus, with whom I still have a great friendship. We were able to remain together throughout the war until we got to Gunskirchen.

Mísa was a boy about my age, maybe a little younger and shorter. Him and his family got deported in December of 1942 and when they got here, he was able to live with his mother in the L425 barrack for a few weeks until they sent him here with us. In June of 1943, he managed to do a very short and secret Bar-Mitzvah.

We got organized in groups of 30 boys and each group had their *Madrich* –leader. Ours was a redhead called Jirí Frankl. He looked like he was in his late twenties, around 28 years old. He was very smart and a good person. Every day he taught us about a different subject, Mondays was algebra, Tuesdays literature, Wednesdays science, Thursdays history, etc. He was always trying to keep us busy, giving us stuff to do. With time, I met and became good friends with many other boys that I remember until this day: Oscar Pick who we used to call *Slunce*-Sun, Petr Beck A.k.a *Bekyñe*-Gypsy, Jirí Hahn - *Honítko*, Ota Wasserman was *Hastros*-Grumpy, Pavel Gross was *Mydlajs*, to name a few… We enjoyed calling each other by our nicknames.

Since my dad knew a lot about food, they put him to work at the butchery along with the butcher. The butcher was also known as "The Hangman" because he offered himself to hang punished prisoners. He told my dad that, for obvious reasons, nobody wanted to have that job and since he mastered the art of killing animals with the least amount of pain and suffering, he thought he was the best one in the camp to do it.

Later, when we left for Auschwitz, he came in the same train with us. When they heard about his story from Terezin, they made him *Kapo* and after a few months he became mentally ill. He acted so crazy that everyone was afraid of him, even my dad.

In March of 1943, after a long winter, farming and agriculture time started and I was among a few lucky kids that were selected to work at the camp garden on top of the city walls. We were planting, growing, and picking various fruits, vegetables, and legumes under the supervision of E. Sonnenschein. The wall that surrounded the camp was a double wall about 33 feet tall and 98 feet apart and filled with soil. I spent several months working there. The Germans wanted to have fertile soil to make it a source of food.

Several times I imagined escaping from there, but it was close to impossible. Not only were we really high up, but we were also constantly watched over, especially so we wouldn't steal any of the fruits and veggies. If someone got caught doing anything like that, they could get a horrible beating, be included in a train to go east or even be immediately hanged. Usually, the Jews were watching their own backs, but they will also take cake of one another.

One of the things we grew there were leeks. Since it was very dangerous to take it to the barracks with us, we were always trying to find opportunities to eat it right there, raw, and dirty but better than nothing. I got used to eating leeks, and even nowadays it is something I love eating, clean and cooked of course, with a piece of bread.

There were also fruit trees. Our job was to collect the fruits and bring them to the Germans. The Germans were only interested in the good, pretty fruits on the trees; the ones that fell on the floor and got bruised or rotten we had permission to eat, so of course we were always helping them fall and letting them get damaged.

Whenever I got to see my parents we talked about food, how bad and how little it was. Our conversations also included speculations about who might come in the next train or who would leave in the following train to the East. When would the war be over? The rumor was always, in three months. Everybody always said, in three months. In the camp there were a few "ghost whisperers" with their kit and tools, and people would take turns going to talk to them and their spirits to ask them about the future, especially about who would win the war and when.

Sometimes a few friends would gather to eat something we found or stole, like a can of sardines, which was precious. I used to store some of those since we thought they wouldn't search the kids barracks. But of course, one day there was a big search conducted by the Germans and they found my sardines among other "valuable" items we had hidden and took everything away. When they left, I wasn't only sad I was really upset, especially at myself. I learned that it was better to eat the food the moment we got it, and not save it for later. At camp you never knew what would happen later.

In mid-October there was a rumor that some prisoners had escaped from the camp, so the Germans decided to do an *Appell,* or a census. We heard they were very common at other concentration camps, but not in Terezin. The way it worked was everyone (except really sick people) had to walk to a nearby valley outside the camp. We couldn't take anything with us, we were just walking in long lines until we got there. They started counting us over and over again, all day. Late that night they told us we could start walking back. Deep inside people were happy, many of them thought we were going to get executed there.

Later that month, I believe on October 29th, 1943, our *Heim* started writing our own weekly magazine called *Kamarád*-Peers. It was a mini, handwritten newspaper narrating what happened that week in the Ghetto and we just passed it around to be read between us. We were trying to imitate a better-known magazine called *Vedem* –See, written by a bigger and more important *Heim* called L-417 or "School". Our magazine was stored in the ceiling behind a beam and was found years later after the war was over. Today it is displayed in a Holocaust Museum in Israel.

KAMARAD NEWSPAPER, NO. 1, COVER

COURTESY OF BEIT THERESIENSTADT, KIBBUTZ GIVAT HAYIM-IHUD, ISRAEL.

It was well known that a train left from Terezin to the East, but no one knew exactly where it was headed. People that arrived in trains before ours were directed to *Treblinka* and there weren't many survivors. People did whatever they could to avoid getting in those trains, especially at the beginning.

It was hard to understand the logic they followed to fill the trains. Sometimes we heard they were taking families with kids so we would all spread apart and kept a low profile for a day or two. Other times they were looking for single individuals, kids with no parents or older people so we would go find our parents and make them notice we were still all together. So, one way or another, with my father working at the butcher place, they kept our entire family and we were able to survive there for a month, two months… thirteen months.

In September of 1943, two trains with twenty-five hundred people left Terezin for Auschwitz. We felt lucky not to be included in those. But in December, I got a note saying I had to present myself on the fifteenth of the same month to the transportation noted as "Dr". My dad, mother and sister got the same note. That day we went to the train loading platform and in alphabetical order they made us get in an animal transportation wagon, with metal bars on every window.

ÚSTŘEDNÍ KARTOTÉKA — TRANSPORTY.

R. č. 51.885

Osers Harry

Rodná data: 1.5.1939

Adresa před deportací: Praha I Dusní 3

HLÁŠEN OPĚT
DO
EVIDENCE

1. transport
dne: 12. XI 194...
č. 476

2. transport
dne: 15.12.1943
číslo: Dr -1530
do: Osvětim

TRANSPORT CARD

When it was my family's turn to board, we started loading our bags and I had to be the first one in (Harry, Maria, Rodolfo, and Sonia), but right after me the wagon filled up and they closed the doors. My parents and sister stayed outside.

Did they get in the next wagon? Were they allowed to stay in Terezin? Were they sent in a different train somewhere else? Did they stay all together, or did they get separated? All these questions started to pop up in my head. I tried to reach the little window to see if I could see them but it was really high up so I couldn't. Then I tried calling them, screaming their names, and trying to hear their voices answering back to me, but there was a lot of noise, many people, most of them doing the same. Some crying, some saying goodbyes, some complaining. I tried everything I could until the train started moving slowly, after that I just found a little corner where I sat and started thinking that from now on, I was going to be alone.

The trip to hell lasted three long days and three awful nights. There wasn't any food or water to begin with, no bathrooms either so you can only imagine the smell. And on top of everything, it was cold. But the worst part was the anxiety, the uncertainty, and the heartache. The idea of being by myself for the first time ever was haunting me. I knew I had it easy back at Terezin, I knew I was lucky. Was I running out of luck now?

IV

DORIT: Scary moments

I clearly remember the tragic day when they came to get us. It was March of 1942; I was six years old. We felt it coming; we heard rumors, our neighbors were leaving one by one. I was excited because my parents had told me we would have to leave in a train, and I was finally going to ride in one! My father got furious, and he yelled at me saying:

> "How can you be so happy? You don't know where they are taking us, or if you are going to like it there!"

We started packing, and my dad told my mom to be smart and think ahead. My mom hid butter and shortening in face cream and toothpaste containers, she hid bags of sugar and canned food in our sleeping bags and coats. The day we went to the train station my mom made me wear three dresses one on top of the other which made me really uncomfortable and stiff. She said we needed to have extras, in case one of them gets ruined, so I didn't complain. Some people grabbed coins and covered them in fabric to use them as buttons.

First, we all had to go to a place called *Schloiska*, where they gathered all the people that were included in certain trains. Just before we left, my mom made my favorite dessert, a chocolate-wafer layer cake called *Pischinger*. I took the last piece with me and held it in my hand the entire way. When we got there, we had to be inspected by the Germans, so my mother told me to hide the cake behind my back and to not mention it. I was so nervous that I started to tighten my hand squeezing the cake and at one point I felt the chocolate melting and dripping through my fingers. The Germans didn't see it, but that was one very scary moment. We spent three days in that place.

When we finally started boarding the train it was dark out. I don't remember if it was late at night or very early in the morning. It was also raining. The Germans walked back and forth with their big scary dogs. I didn't like those dogs. The SS men were wearing their black rubber coats and their black boots, and it made a lot of squeaky noises under the rain, it's a sound I will never forget.

That moment I remember my mother telling me:

"Look around you, look at everything so you would remember later all we had to go through".

I don't remember how long the trip was either. For me it was just a train ride. We arrived at a train station; I believed it was called Bohusovice. As soon as we got out from the train a few men started yelling at us:

"Men to this side, women and children to this side"

They made us form lines of five people each and we started walking toward Theresienstadt's Ghetto. Terezin used to be a military city that the Germans started using as a concentration camp when the War started. The first couple of days they sent us to a barrack for military garrison, and I was able to stay with my mom. We couldn't go anywhere else. After three days they moved us to a bigger barrack called *Dresdner Kaserne*. It had three internal patios. We went directly to one of the patios where they had five tables set up with people registering all the inmates and telling them in what room they were staying. My room number was AE312, when my mom and I got to it, we realized we were sharing it with eleven other women. The room was about thirteen square feet.

7 Years Old Portrait of Dorit

Illustrated by a Terezin Prisoner. 1943

V

HARRY: Best of the worst.

On September 8, 1943, the September trains arrived at Auschwitz II- Birkenau, bringing five thousand and seven inmates from Terezin. These trains became the nucleus of the newly created *Familienlager BIIb* camp –Family camp. In this section of Auschwitz, for the first time there were both men, women and children, although they slept in separate barracks. Kids up to fifteen years old were staying at a special barrack, supervised by Freddy Hirsch.

Until then, the general procedure at Auschwitz main camp was to keep only the strong men and a few women from each transport and the rest (most of them) were ordered to stripped naked in large "shower" rooms and after the gates were closed and sealed, they would release the gas that would kill all of them at once. Then they used crematoriums to burn the bodies.

The *Familienlager* was the first and only camp of its type in Auschwitz, created specifically to receive Jewish people coming from Terezin. It was probably used as propaganda to show to outsiders and to receive visits from the Red Cross when they came to do inspections of the concentration camp conditions.

On December 17, 1943, we arrived in Auschwitz II- Birkenau / *Familienlager*. I was 14 years old. Two December trains "Dr" and "Ds" carrying twenty-five hundred Jews each. I didn't know it but my good friend Mísa, and my counselor Jirí, were traveling with me in those same trains, along with other acquaintances.

When we were getting close to Auschwitz, the train slowed down and I looked through the wagon's little window and saw a bunch of lights in a line, and I assumed it was a street, but when we came closer, I realized it was a barbed wire fence surrounding the camp; there were signs all over it showing a skull illustration with the following message:

HALT! Lebensgefährlich! Hochspannung!

STOP! Deathly Dangerous! High Voltage!

Suddenly the train came to a complete stop. All the wagon doors opened at the same time.

"Raus, Schnell!" – OUT, QUICK!!

Yelled the German officers, and we were forced to get out by means of hits and pushes. People desperately screamed looking for friends and family members. Others just rushed out looking to breathe a little fresh air. Some carried their bags, coats or kids in their hands. Anything you couldn't carry was left in the train and never given back. Once on the platform I could finally see the rest of my family coming out from another wagon, and a little further away I also saw some friends.

The main entrance of the camp had a huge metal gate with a signed that read:

"Arbeit Macht Frei"
"Work Makes (you) Free"

"Arbeit Macht Frei"

AUSCHWITZ. 2010

AUSCHWITZ. 2010

I was very impressed at first with the German Shepherds, yes, the dogs. They were big animals or at least they looked big to me. Always barking, they seemed like they were always mad at us. I was very afraid of them, and very respectful too.

My first priority was to get reunited with my family. So, I started walking as fast as I could, getting in between the people and yelling their names until we found each other. We all hugged. My mom started crying.

After the excitement of the moment, I realized I left my bag inside the wagon. I wanted to get it so I turned around and told my dad I would go back quickly and grab it but he didn't let me. He said that could upset the Germans and we never wanted to do that. I was really upset with myself. I felt guilty and disappointed but that only lasted a few hours, since later that day we realized we would lose all our luggage anyways.

In our same train, traveled Jacob Edelstein, the Terezin chairman of the *Judenrat* (Jewish council) and his entire family. We recognized them when they got off the wagon. But something didn't look right. The Germans took all of them to the side, separate from where all the other passengers were going. We could still see them standing in line when suddenly we heard the shots. They shot and killed each one of them right then, in front of everybody, without any explanation. It was a horrible scene.

Nobody knew what they had done to deserve that, but the Germans didn't need a specific reason to kill Jews. Later on, we heard that the order came from the Germans at Terezin; they thought the Edelstein's knew too much information and had to be silenced forever.

We were taken to the *Familienlager* camp. They separated men from women and kids. They took us to the sauna outside the camp, where they made us undress completely and then shower in groups. They gave us our clothes back, and on our way out, they made us wait in line to get our respective prisoner number tattooed on our left arm. I got the number 169086. It was a peculiar number since depending upon which side it was being read it could be a different number, so if looked from the outside I was inmate 169086 and from the inside I could be 980691. This saved my life on numerous occasions, and almost got me killed once.

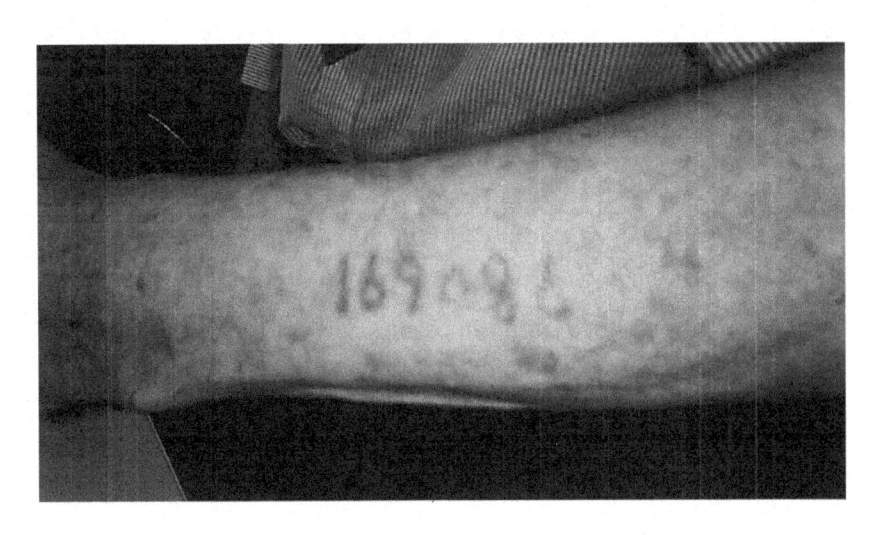

MY NUMBER TATTOO MANY YEARS LATER.

169086

That day, I saw kids of all different ages but one in particular got my attention. It was a little boy; he was probably eighteen months old. He could barely walk or talk, and he was all alone so I took him with me and helped him get undressed, showered, and dressed again, risking getting punished for it. I remember when we got back to the barracks his mom was there and when she saw him, she ran toward us and started yelling at me for losing one of his socks.

In Auschwitz, the main physician was the feared Dr. Josef Mengele. He was later known for performing cruel and sometimes deadly experiments on prisoners for genetic research. He was also in charge of selecting which prisoners would be sent to the gas chambers. I remember he used an L shaped wooden stick. Kids had to stand in front of it and whoever was shorter than the stick was sooner or later sent to the gas chambers. After my little friend stood under it, he was never seen again.

The *Familenlager* camp was very different from the other sub-camps at Auschwitz. One of the many "special treatments" we received was the fact that they never cut our hair off. Also, we were able to wear our regular clothes. All the other Auschwitz inmates wore black and white striped uniforms and had shaved heads. But, like the rest of them we also had our identifying cloth triangle sewn to our clothing below our prisoner number. The different colors classified the type of prisoner: Green- criminal; red- political; black- military, purple- homosexual; yellow-

Jewish. Inside the triangle, a letter identified the nationality. A Jew could have a yellow triangle over an inverted triangle of a different color, forming a star and meaning the person wasn't only Jewish but also a criminal or political prisoner for example.

No other sub-camp had men, women and kids at the same time. We got a hot drink in the morning, but no breakfast, and a thin meatless vegetable soup at noon. In the evening we received a small ration of moldy bread. Most importantly we didn't go through a "selection" process for a long time. Mainly because they were expecting the Red Cross to show up at any moment, like they did at Terezin. They were trying to keep a group of people in decent shape to show off. It's not surprising that the survival rate at the *Familienlager* was much higher than at the rest of the Auschwitz camp and other extermination camps. The Red Cross never came.

PHOTO BY JOSE DANIEL URDANETA BALLESTEROS

MEAL PORTION SERVING CUP

What was most shocking to us wasn't the Germans or the Polish at the *Familienlager*, but the first five thousand Terezin Jews. It only took three months of living there to harshen them and contaminate them with hatred. They thought since we were left at Terezin three months more than them, we were so fortunate. They were in charge of the barracks, and they treated us really badly. It was very uncomfortable and unpleasant for us. And since we didn't know exactly what was going on at Auschwitz, they made sure we got informed fast and clear:

"Do you see the black smoke coming out of those chimneys? It's all dead people. That's how you get out of Auschwitz".

Finally, I went to my barrack with the kids my age. The older kids tried teaching us algebra, arithmetic, writing, etc. with little to no paper, we did what we could.

At Birkenau, the barracks were designed to be horse stables. On one end, the main entrance, there was a cubicle where the person in charge would keep the list of names and numbers of every prisoner. At the other end of the room the people in charge had a little more room for themselves to sleep "comfortably". Of course, no prisoner was allowed in any of these places.

Inside the barracks, everything was completely symmetrical. There was a fireplace located in the middle of the building with ducts extending to both ends of the barrack, ending in a chimney. On each side of the building there were three floor bunk beds one next to the other. They were two meters wide, and they would usually fit six people per floor. On top of the wooden panels there was a thin straw mattress.

Sometimes the panels would give up and brake, and everything would fall on top of the people below. It was very uncomfortable. When it rained, we had leaks in the roof, and we didn't have any kind of insulation, so it was wet, really cold in the wintertime and always dirty. We saw rats all the time.

The chimney ducts were often used for punishments, the prisoner had to lay on top of it and the Germans would hit them with big sticks. Everyone else had to watch.

The barracks were located twenty meters from one another; but it wasn't easy to communicate in between them. I ran into my parents and sister a few times while walking in the camp, but we couldn't speak much. Our *Lageraltester*, camp supervisor, was called Arno Bohm. He was a German prisoner who wore the number eight and a green star, which meant he was a police prisoner or in other words, a criminal. The camp's commander-in-chief was an *SS-Lagerfuhrer* named Buntruck. Because he was so robust, we used to call him "Bulldog". Our leader, Freddy Hirsch, was a young, tall, good-looking guy who we esteemed and admired a lot. He was a German Jew who lived in Czechoslovakia since he was twenty years old, so he spoke Czech with a German accent. He planned activities for us to teach us about discipline, cleanness, and self-esteem.

At this camp, life was relatively calm. We had to wake up every day at 4:30 a.m. with the siren sound or with a "Gong" hit, except Sundays when they woke us up at 5:30 a.m. and some winter days at 6:00 a.m. Right after we had to do the infamous prisoner count known as *Appel* where the *Campfuhrer* would yell:

"Zu Fünf Anstellen," - FORM LINES OF FIVE!!

All the prisoners would be organized so he could start counting us. We would do the *Appel* two times a day, early morning and in the afternoon, when everyone returned from work. If any prisoner appeared to be missing, the *Appel* would last hours, no matter the weather conditions. It could be raining, snowing, super sunny and hot or frigid cold, and we would be standing there without moving while the Germans looked for the missing person, or just as punishment.

The adults would always go to work, and kids could do different activities. My group used to play chess with wooden pieces we made ourselves by cutting and carving fallen branches. We also played ping-pong and soccer. We even organized soccer tournaments among the different barracks because the SS loved this sport and enjoyed watching us play.

The food would come in a big barrel, and we had to form a line holding our container so we could receive a little bit of soup and a piece of bread a day. I remember people, me included, asking to get soup from the bottom of the barrel, since that was where you could find the majority of the solid substance, but only sometimes you would get some.

In the camp there was a very peculiar way for guards to send messages. If they wanted to tell someone to be at a certain place for example, they would say it and add the words "*weiter geben!*" which means Repeat! So, all the prisoners around the guard would yell the same thing and every prisoner who heard the words would yell again and so on until the message would get to the person it was intended for.

It was common for the SS to call a prisoner just so when he showed up, they would take his hat and throw it far away. Then they would ask the prisoner to go get it fast. When the prisoner started running, they would shoot him in the back saying he was trying to escape. They used to play this "game" a lot when the female SS were around so they could show off in front of them. That's why every time I saw an SS next to a woman, I would try to elude them somehow.

The night of March 7th, 1944, all the 3,800 remaining prisoners from the original 5,007 September trains population, (the ones before mine) had to be transferred to the next-door camp BIIa; exactly six months after their arrival to Birkenau; with the justification of sending them to a place with better conditions and making more room in the crowded *Familienlager*. Some people were hopeful, others didn't believe it and were really fearful so there was a lot of confusion but there was nothing anybody could do.

Hundreds of drunk SS guards came with their dogs to get all these prisoners out of the barracks and into the transports. Families tried to stay together but everybody was being pushed around and torn apart. There was a lot of screaming, crying, begging, dogs barking, it was dark out. Among the four thousand prisoners, about six hundred were children. Freddy Hirsch was one of them too. When they all left, there was complete silence, nobody talked, and we all went to bed.

The following night we heard that they were all assassinated in the gas chambers. They made up almost half of the camp's population. Only a few lives were spared, a set of twins and a few sick people that were in the hospital at the time, I think less than ten total.

In those days, not only you would hear the rumors spreading all over the camp, but you could also see and smell the huge black smoke columns elevating from the crematorium chimneys; A dark and heavy smoke covering the sky impregnating the air with a smell of burned skin and hair. Some days were worse than others, but I would remember that smell for years. Some people would say we were next. "Your only way out of here is through the chimney!" I heard it more than once.

So, we kept thinking that at any time they would put us on a train and we would be sent to the gas chambers like the others. It was a rough time. Slowly everyone went back to their routine. But the truth was we didn't have many days left at the *FamilienLager*.

On April 6th, 1944, the prisoner Vitezlav Lederer escaped, helped by the *SS Rottenfuhrer* Victor Pestek. His intentions were to let people at Theresienstadt, and the rest of the world know about the Jewish situation at the death camp of KL Auschwitz and the foreseeable, sad, and deadly future of the December trains population still back at the camp.

Lederer and Pestek were very lucky to escape successfully. After looking all night, the Germans couldn't find them. So, the following day they had such indignation that they decided to publicly hang two people from the barrack they belonged to. However, the rumor at the camp was that Pestek had fallen in love with a Jewish girl from the camp, and indeed a few weeks later he came back to Auschwitz to try to rescue her. Unfortunately, Pestek wasn't so lucky this time around and he got caught by the Germans. After giving him a very bad public beating, they killed him.

Three more trains from Terezin arrived at Auschwitz in May of 1944 to fill the now half empty *Familienlager*. *Dz, Ea* and *Eb* with a total of 7,503 Jews from different nationalities. Around one third was from Czechoslovakia and the rest from Germany, Austria, and Holland. Now us, the December population, were in charge of "welcoming" them and supervising the barracks.

We weren't cruel or mean to them, we didn't treat them the way the September trains inmates treated us. They found a place in the barracks and like us, were also able to keep their hair. They were assigned new numerical series starting with an A or B to distinguish between Jews and non-Jews.

In June of 1944, exactly six months after our arrival at Birkenau, the December train population was threatened and predetermined for a collective assassination in the gas chambers, and we knew it.

VI
DORIT: My life in the camp

I don't recall many details of my life in that barrack. I know in our room there were women from all different nationalities. I could hear people talking in Czech, German, and Hungarian. We slept on thin little mattresses organized one next to the other, with no space in between.

If we had followed the rules, I would have been sent away to a kinder barrack where all the little kids like me were situated without their parents. But my mom did everything in her power to keep me with her. That actually saved my life because shortly after, all the kids from the Kinder barracks were sent in one train straight to the gas chambers.

While at the camp, I lost a few teeth and got some new permanent ones. But it was really painful because they were growing weak and usually got infected right away. One day, I woke up really hot and sweaty, not feeling good at all. They sent me to the hospital and said I had contracted scarlet fever. When I got to the hospital, one of the nurses started checking me and out of nowhere she got a shaving machine and started shaving my hair. I couldn't say anything; I was too weak to stop them or even ask why. I just sat there looking at my blond curls falling off my head to my shoulders and then to the floor until there wasn't any left. When she was done, she gave me striped pajamas to wear. I could feel the tears running down my cheeks, but I stayed silent.

I had to stay in the hospital for six weeks. It was the first time I was away from my mother. I was scared, lonely and not feeling good, so I cried a lot until one day I saw one of my cousins at the hospital, who was also sick. He told me stories and jokes that made me feel better, and he stayed with me most of the day.

I remember there was a little window at the top of my room, it had metal bars, but you could see some green leaves from a neighbor tree peaking in. I really missed seeing flowers and plants. We used to say whenever that tree changed its leaves, the war would be over, and we would be able to go back home. But many seasons passed before that happened.

Finally, when I was healthy enough to be released, my mom came to pick me up. A few other kids and I went outside and standing in front of her, she asked one of them if he could please go back inside to find me. I had to yell:

"Mommy it's me Dorit, I'm right here".

Her face, although a little shocked at first to see me so skinny and bold, lighted up. She started to cry while giving me a big hug.

Without knowing it, getting sick was the second time my life had been spared, since at that moment they wouldn't send divided families to the Death camps. We couldn't see my dad for months, maybe a year. He couldn't leave his barrack, even though it didn't have a wired fence around it. Most of the Terezin guards came from the *Judenrat*. There was a police squad named *Ghettowache* who was in charge of maintaining order in the camp. Each sector had their lookouts. They came running when they saw the Germans so we would be prepared. Some men working temporarily near our barracks would secretly bring us goods, and if a German came while they were still with us, we had to hide them the best we could under a bed.

PAPER MONEY USED AT TEREZIN

My dad managed to find a job in the electricity building as the main engineer. Sometimes he would have to come near our barracks to make repairs. Someone would quickly tell my mom where they saw him working and my mom would go out running to try to find him and see if she could talk to him for at least a couple of minutes.

They found a perfect hiding place to meet and talk, the coal depot. Although a little dirty, it was dark and quiet. My mom told me one time they almost got caught by a German.

Time passed and my mom got sick with dysentery. She lost a lot of weight. She was barely eighty pounds. I was always trying to get extra food for us, and sometimes people felt bad for me and gave me a little more than usual. One time, I spoke to the person who served the soup and asked him if he could get my mom a job in the kitchen. He told me to find my mom and bring her over. When he saw her so skinny, he didn't want to give her a job thinking she would be too weak to work, but my mom convinced him she could. From then on, my mom left for work at four in the morning and came back at ten at night, when I was already asleep.

We didn't have time to speak much anymore, and when we did it was generally reprimanding me for things I did wrong during the day. The other women in the room wanted me gone to the kid's quarter (since I was only a burden for them) and they were always watching over me to criticize my behavior and tell my mom about it.

I got into big trouble one time because I ate my entire sugar portion (a tiny bag for the entire week) and some from my mom's portion in one sitting. The women were furious, saying how irresponsible that was and told my mom I deserved a spanking. My mom had to do it. Other times, they would yell at me for listening to conversations not meant to be heard by little girls.

Outside the room, I could practically do whatever I wanted since no one was paying attention to me. I often went to the old people's barracks and traded them soup for bread, since the bread was usually too hard for them to bite. They would try to teach us how to read and write in Hebrew, and I was able to learn some basic letters and sounds.

I was very observant of everything happening in the camp. I would pay special attention to the arrival of the provisions and supplies trucks. Sometimes, if I was lucky, I saw something fall off and I could quickly pick it from the floor and hide it, like a bar of soap or a can of food. But slowly I realized that there weren't many kids my age in the camp; I was an exception. So, if I drew too much attention to myself and a German guard realized it, I could be taken away... forever. I started to go out less and had to be really quiet and careful not to disturb anyone.

VII
HARRY: Saved by "The Angel of Death"

It was the end of June 1944; a little after the arrival of the new May trains that we realized that the *Familienlager* BIIb camp would come to an end. I was fifteen years old. Among other things, the Germans realized that the Red Cross would never come so there wasn't a need for a camp like this. So BIIB was shut down, as they would close down every other camp: with the dreaded "selections."

For the first round, they chose the strongest, most hard-working men to go to Schwarzheide. Then a second round of less strong, older men, where my dad was included, was sent first to section

BIIa of our camp, and then fourteen days later were transported to Blechhammer, a KL Auschwitz dependent camp where they were fabricating synthetic gas.

During a third selection, they chose strong working women to send to Hamburgo-Neuengamme; both my mom and my sister were selected here. At this moment we were able to say goodbye. It was short and fast, I didn't have the opportunity to think about feelings, or I just don't remember how I felt. No time for that. So, by now, there were only kids, teenagers fifteen and under, and seniors over fifty years old left at BIIB.

After a few days at our almost empty camp, the infamous Doctor Mengele came to visit us and made one last selection at our barracks. I remember we had to pull our pants down and walk in front of him, one by one, and with a small movement of his right hand he would send kids to the left (the chosen ones) or to the right (the ones staying). In the meantime, his assistant would write down in a notebook the numbers of the chosen kids. When it was my turn, he sent me to the left, and while I was walking past the assistant, I noticed he didn't write my number correctly. I bravely, and very politely, asked him to correct it and luckily, he did, because if he hadn't, my real number wouldn't have been on that list, and I would have had to stay.

Two hours after our selection, they transferred us to the neighboring Men's camp, the Manner Lager BIId, also in Birkenau. We had a feeling, almost certainty that the group that wasn't chosen was going straight to the gas chamber, although sometimes we weren't sure what group was "the chosen one." The night of July 11, 1944, we heard the news that the remaining people at *Familienlager* BIIb camp were mass murdered in the gas chambers.

That's how we became a group of young kids "saved" at the last minute by the man known as "The Angel of Dead." Forty-five years later, my mate and friend Johnny Freund referred to us as the *Birkenau Boys*.

There is a lot of speculation around the reason for this last selection. Personally, I always believed that the *Lagerfuhrer*, German director of the Manner Lager BIId camp, who I thought wasn't a mean man, had said he had some space in his barracks and could use a hundred of the best shaped kids to do messenger jobs and that kind of labor.

Some want to believe that our friends Helmuth Szpryzer and Ota Furth spoke up and interceded with Mengele to help us, which I think is VERY unlikely. Others think the Dr. wanted to run more experiments on the strongest kids left in the camp but never got to it. Maybe it was pure luck, or a mix of the previous reasons.

The truth is that I was one of the last ones to leave the *Familienlager* and one of the very few that survived it, probably by chance.

In the Manner Lager they accommodated us in barrack number thirteen, who's *Blockalteste*, chief of barracks, was Emil Bednarek. This barrack was the "*Straffblock*" or punishment barrack inside the camp. It was used to reprimand people that tried to escape or deserved some kind of punishment for their actions. We weren't there for that reason, but it was the place where they had room available. On the patio outside the barrack, there was among other things, a wooden box with an opening in the floor used for hanging inmates.

We immediately got all of our hair cut and shaved. There were Jews and non-Jews from many different nationalities. We were doing all kinds of jobs, from practical useful things like pushing a cartwheel full of things from one place to another, feeding horses, cleaning and removing snow when necessary, to small, stupid pointless things like digging a hole and filling it right back up.

One day in July, just a few days after we got to BIId, the Germans caught two Jewish inmates that had escaped. As punishment, we all had to wake up super early and do an extra census. Later that day, the two men had to march around the camp holding a sign that read:

"HURRA!, wir sind schon wieder da"

"HOORAY!, we are back again"

After that, they were sent to our barracks where they received an awful beating from the Germans. We were all forced to watch. Their bodies turned purple, then red, then black. Their skin was open, raw and their faces disfigured. For a couple of days, they had to crawl to work like that and when they got better the guards received an order to hang them. The hanging would take place in the main plaza and again, everyone had to watch. It was a horrible scene.

After spending a week in this camp, I was starting to notice how things worked here, and I realized the leader of the camp named Wolf didn't seem like a bad person. He used to ride his bike every day around the camp, so one day I gathered all my courage and went to talk to him. After a proper salute, I asked him if I could work as the *Packet Stelle Laufer*, "mail office messenger," where they received, opened and censored all the packages sent to the camp inmates. He asked me:

"Do they need you over there?"

To which I responded a quick and firm "YES", even though I had never been in the mail office and had no idea if they really needed anyone. So he replied:

"If that is the case, you have my permission"

Wolf kept slowly riding his bike and I walked right beside him. When we got to barrack number two, where there was a lateral entrance to the mail office, he turned right and entered. I walked behind him. Once inside, he asked if they needed a messenger. The manager saw me beside him and supposed that I was his protégée that he was trying to allocate, so he quickly answered:

"Yes, he could start immediately"

I was so relieved that my plan worked out, but since I knew that they really didn't need anyone, I tried to make myself useful right away to secure my new job. I grabbed a broom that I saw in a corner and started sweeping the place. While doing this, I found a chess game on a shelf. I ask aloud who wanted to play; for a moment no one said anything, until I heard a very hoarse voice say:

"I can play."

He was the *Packetstelle-schreiber*, the second in command in the mail office. We sat down at a little table in the middle of the office, where he arranged the game and next to it, he put a bag of chocolate confectionery. He told me:

"If you can win, the chocolates are yours"

The last time I ate chocolate was three years prior, so you can imagine my excitement. Everyone in the office gathered around us to watch the match. My heart was racing, but I tried to hide my emotions. I played the best I could with my nerves. After an intense match, I couldn't believe it but I won! I still don't know, and I guess I never will, if I genuinely won or if he let me win because he was a much better player than me and he won most of our other matches. Regardless, by winning this game not only did I get to keep the bag of chocolates, but I also secured my job in the mail office and even maybe saved my own life. I was able to stay there until my last day in Auschwitz with better food and treatment than anywhere else.

In the mail office, they were all Polish, and I was the only Jew. But for some reason they were all protective of me. At some point they even asked me to move into their barrack with them and so a little later they moved me from barrack thirteen to number four, the one next to the mail office where I stayed until my last day in Birkenau.

My job as a messenger consisted of notifying all the barracks when the shipment of packages was ready. I also had to take notes on which prisoner received a package and when. These notes were taken in Polish, so I had to quickly learn how to read, speak and write numbers in Polish. Most of the packages were for Germans and Polish people.

We had to open every envelope and package that arrived at the camp. We had to confiscate letters that could contain any information about the camps. We also confiscated (and kept) any food that needed to be cooked since it was forbidden to do so at the camp. Any package sent to a deceased person we would also keep, that's how while working there, I had access to extra food and other forbidden things.

One day, while working outside the office, the second selection of men from our *Familenlager* walked by our camp on their way to Blechhammer. I could see all the men marching while holding in their hands a big rock to be used for the pavement of the *Lagerstrasse* – Main Street. One of them was my dad.

When I recognized him, I quickly ran to the office and asked the Polish men to give me a piece of bread and butter to give to my dad, they agreed and gave me the bread, so I quickly ran back out to hand him the food. I managed to find him in the line again. I knew I had to be really careful not to touch the electric fence that would electrocute me in seconds; but I was able to pass the bread to him without guards watching; he grabbed it and put it in his pocket, he picked up his rock and kept walking. With this gesture, not only was I helping him but also telling him not to worry about me, I was doing ok.

I stood there for a couple of minutes, watching how he walked away, and then he turned his head back and with a gesture of his face he said goodbye. That was the last time I saw my dad.

A few days later, cleaning and moving packages around, a whole rack fell down with all kinds of confiscated items and files with letters and records. Unfortunately, my leg got caught under the cabinet. When the polish helped me up, we could see my bloody left foot, with a cut almost down to the bone. I suddenly felt a shooting pain and felt cold. Two Polish men walked me to the infirmary where a doctor cleaned the wound and gave me a paper bandage. One hour later, I went back limping to the mail office to keep working, since my biggest fear was for them to replace me, leaving me wounded and unemployed.

Everything was going relatively well. I was still in pain, but healing. Unfortunately, three days after my accident there was another selection headed again by none other than Dr. Mengele. Of course, I was still hurting and limping, which was extremely disadvantageous and dangerous because if the Dr. realized it and thought I was weak or handicapped, he would send me right to the gas chambers.

Every time there was a selection, it was mandatory to put your pants down, so they could inspect the entire naked body for lesions, rashes, etc. The Polish heard about this selection in advance and warned me, so I decided to take all my bandages off since it would definitely draw attention to the wound. When it was all off, I could still see some of the bone, so I wasn't sure if it was the best thing to do.

The time for the selection arrived and with nerves of steel I stood in line. When I dropped my pants, I made sure they bunched up around the wound, covering it and when I started walking, I exaggerated the limp or improperly walked like blaming the pants around my ankles for it. It was the perfect excuse! When Mengele saw me, he sent me to the right, saving my life one more time.

In both August and September of 1944, several trains from the Litzmannstadt ghetto arrived at our neighbor camp BIIe. Between the barbed wire fences, I could recognize Dr. Zunterstain among the new prisoners, he was one of my uncles. I ran towards him to say hi, he told me my other uncle Pavel Osers was also with him in the same train. They were both deported in October of 1941 from Prague to Litzmannstadt. Just as I did with my dad, I ran to the mail office, grabbed two pieces of bread, went back, and threw it to them above the fence. They received it with a big smile and walked away. I never saw them again.

New trains also arrived to BIId from Theresienstadt, and among them some friends and family members, like my cousin Jiri Gross, who ultimately survived. I tried to send them extra food when I could, but none of them were even tattooed since they were quickly transferred to other camps or straight to gas chambers. No one wanted to believe what we told them about Auschwitz and the terrible destiny of most prisoners.

One day, I was watching a group of ten-year-old kids from Ukraine who found some very weak and hungry prisoners laying against a barrack. The kids offered them their piece of bread but in return they had to let themselves get beaten by the kids the way the Germans did. The prisoners accepted. I don't know if the kids thought it was some kind of funny game or if they were just getting used to being surrounded by violence and cruelty. But the whole scene was definitely an example of the morale and priorities of people living in the camp. People were getting desperate; hunger chased prisoners twenty-four seven, 365 days a year.

Days and weeks passed. At the end of October 1944, the prisoners working at the crematorium planned a coup where they set one building on fire and killed a couple of SS; they ran everywhere. Unfortunately, all of them got caught, were tortured, and then killed. After the incident, the Germans realized that for the Polish it was easier to escape since they spoke the same language as the villages around them and many even had family nearby, so they decided to deport all the Polish prisoners to camps in other countries. Of course, this included my Polish friends from the mail office.

Every time prisoners were deported to other camps, they had to go through an inspection with the goal of confiscating any valuables they wanted to take with them. All my friends asked me to hold their valuables, like watches and other pieces of jewelry, while getting inspected so I could give it back afterwards. Risking my own life, I accepted the task since I wanted to return all the favors they did for me. On their way out I ran to them and returned everything they had given me. They totally deserved it.

They assigned a couple of new people to work at the mail office, but we started getting less and less mail and there wasn't much work to do anymore. I imagined they would close our office soon after.

VIII
DORIT: The war garden

To receive your food portion, you had to go to the distribution place at the patio. You had to bring your bowl, form a line, and wait patiently. After you received your portion, you had to take good care of it! I would always try to do two different lines so I could get double portions, but it did not always work.

For breakfast, we would get some sort of coffee, for lunch a watered-down soup and for dinner soup again and maybe a piece of stale bread too. Since my mom was working in the kitchen, she would often bring something extra to eat. For example, one of my mom's duties in the kitchen was to peel potatoes, so she would try to peel extra thick layers of skin and put them in her pockets, then when she got to our room, we would cook them with an electric stove that my dad found for us. In our room, there was a sixteen-year-old girl who worked at the gardens on top of the camp's wall, and sometimes she would bring leek leaves that we cooked along with the potato skins. It made a much better soup! But I was still very hungry. Everyone was, all the time.

I remember the mother of that girl promised me that when the war was over, she would invite me over to her house and cook a chicken and potato dish or a beef stew, but unfortunately, none of them survived.

The room mattresses were full of bugs and lice. In the summer, with the heat and itchiness, young people would take them outside and sleep on the patio with a little fresh air. When my mom was asleep, I would also take my mattress out and sleep outside. She was too weak to do it. The young people outside used to tell stories and sing, and for me it was an adventure every night.

One day, I needed to use the latrine and when I opened the door a woman fell out of it. She was dead. At first, I was really scared, but the image engraved in my head was even worse. I tried closing my eyes, but she was still there, and it wouldn't go away. From that day on, I hated the latrine and refused to use it. I would hold it until the last second and if there wasn't any other possible option, I would double check outside and inside and then go in very carefully. My mom felt bad for me and since I was little, she tried to find me a small container so I could pee in the room. But that was also a problem for us since none of the other women liked it.

At some point you were able to go from one barrack to another. My dad shared a room with my uncle who was a doctor. Sometimes, when my uncle was on call, my dad invited me to sleep with him. There were a lot of other men there but I liked sleeping there because they had three level beds. Also, my dad would make me something extra to eat and even some tea. Sometime later, the Germans moved us to the electrician barracks and both my mom, and I got to be with my dad.

I loved walking towards a little plaza in front of the German head offices that had a bunch of beautiful flowers. I admired all of the different colors and sizes. I had not forgotten the beating I took from my dad over the stolen flowers of our neighbor back home, but one day I couldn't resist the temptation. I made sure no one was around or looking, so I could grab a couple of flowers to plant close to where I lived. Thankfully, this time nobody noticed.

With these flowers and help from another boy, I could make my little garden outside the electrician's building.

IX

HARRY: The odyssey

That same December, the Germans decided to close the mail office in KL Auschwitz II Birkenau as expected. From now on, all the mail censorship would be done at Auschwitz I, the main camp. Luckily, the director of the *Packet Stelle* there loved to show off and wanted to have his own personal messenger, so he requested for me to be transferred there immediately. I had to walk to the other camp (approximately 2 miles) along with one other SS soldier.

In Auschwitz I, I was placed in the mail barracks again, which was truly an elite place. They all treated me very well. The mail director even had a new suit custom made for me with English fabrics. They also gave me some great tall leather boots. It was a shame that during the three years I spent at Auschwitz, so little of it was spent there. It only lasted until mid-January 1945.

In our mail office we received packages destined to all the subordinates' camps, including Blechhammer, where I knew my father was. I was planning to prepare and send him a fake package, but I never had time. A little after my arrival there, the Russian Army got too close to us, and the Germans decided to shut down both KL Auschwitz I and Blechhammer.

From Auschwitz, the Germans sent daily trains and "dead marches" headed west. On these dead marches, people who couldn't keep up the pace and stayed behind the group were shot in the back of the neck and left there. The same was done to people that fell down and wouldn't get up quickly.

The director of the mail office, among some others, hoped we could stay in Auschwitz until the Russians arrived and made plans for us to hide so we wouldn't be deported. When he told us the plan, I didn't understand it well and went outside of the office. He ran after me quickly and he smacked me in the face so hard I thought I was bleeding. He explained that the longer we could stay in Auschwitz the better it would be for us, so we really had to try not to be seen. We went back inside and hid for a couple of days. When there were only a few people left in the camp, they came looking for us and made us leave. It was

January 21st, and we were part of the last march of inmates that left Auschwitz towards Leslau.

On our way, we could hear in the distance behind us, the sound of machine guns and canyon shots. Auschwitz I was liberated by the Russian army a week after we left, on January 27th of 1945, considered today by the United Nations as the "International Holocaust Remembrance Day." Sometime later, I heard the news that my father had been shot to death between January 21st and 23rd of 1945, during the march that left from Blechhammer to Gross Rosen.

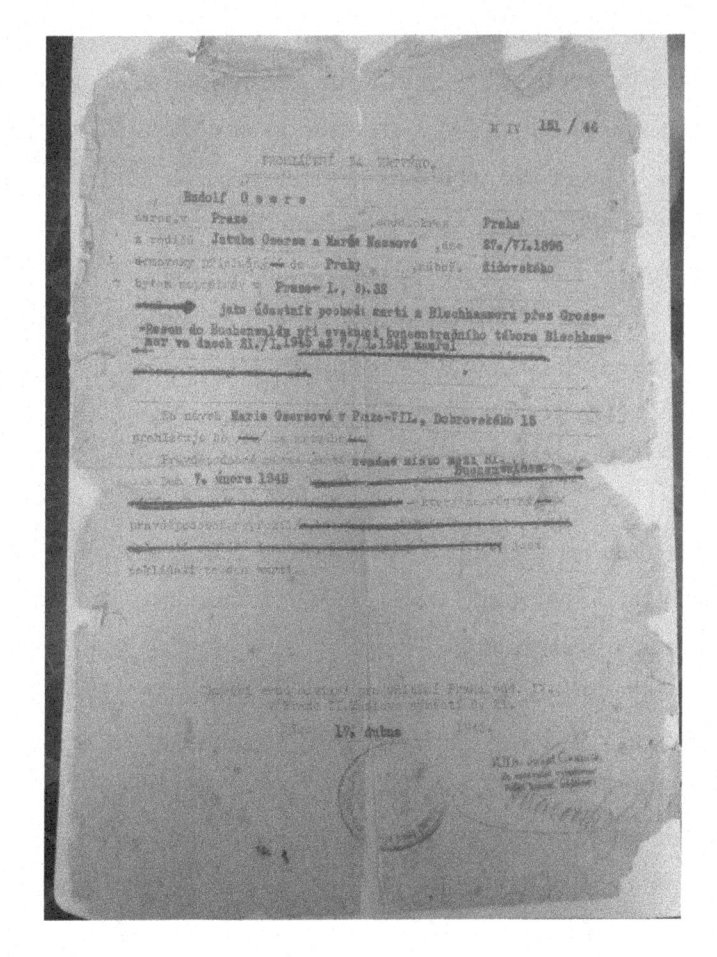

RUDOLF OSERS DEATH CERTIFICATE

AS A PARTICIPANT IN THE DEATH MARCH FROM
BLECHHAMMER THROUGH GROSS-ROSEN TO
BUCHENWALD DURING THE EVACUATION OF THE
BLECHHMNER CONCENTRATION CAMP FROM
21.1.1945 TO 7.2.1945

Our mail office group found an old four-wheeled wagon where we put our belongings and pushed it along with us. We walked all day and would pick up "useful" stuff we found on the way. Some German soldiers saw the wagon and decided to also put their stuff in it so we would push it for them. We didn't mind the extra weight since they started walking by our side, and in a way protected us. The first night, one of the wheels lost a screw and we had to repair it, which put us about a half a mile behind the rest of the group. The German soldiers stayed with us and made the whole convoy stop and wait until we could catch up again.

I have to admit that until that moment I was very lucky to be where I was. That night, we made it to a little town, and we were able to sleep in a shed. The next morning our wagon wasn't there, and our group disbanded. I decided to run to the front of the line and always stay there, since I knew that the ones that stayed behind were killed; so walking at the front would always give me a chance to slow down or rest without getting to the dangerous end of the line.

While walking, I found one of my friends from Birkenau. We walked together for two more days until we made it to Leslau, where they put us in a cattle train without roofs. In other wagons, traveled the rest of the surviving Birkenau boys.

I remember when we passed through the village of Moravská Ostrava, where the people threw food at us from a bridge that our train was parked under. When the Germans realized it, they started shooting at the people on the bridge to scare them away, they wounded and killed a couple of Czech citizens. It was the only time people from the towns helped us.

We continued our trip for three more days. There was a huge snowstorm, so we got cold and wet. I think we passed through Prague, but I'm not sure. We finally got to another camp named Mauthausen in Austria, near Linz.

In Mauthausen, we followed the same routine as in any other concentration camp. They gave us a shower and new numbers; this time the numbers were stamped on a metal sheet that we had to tie with a metal string to our left wrist. Mine was KLM 117137 and it was valid for the other subordinate camps like Melk and Gunskirchen. They took everything we owned, except for some reason I'm still not sure, my good boots.

There I reunited with my friends, the other Birkenau boys. With us, also from BIID, was a group of young non-Jewish boys from Poland and Ukraine. They didn't like us and treated us really badly.

Nights at Mauthausen were horrific. They would constantly yell at us to lay on the floor like sardines, one next to another, the head of one next to the feet of the other and then they would cover us with big communal blankets. You couldn't get up in the middle of the night to go to the bathroom. We stayed there for three days and then we were again deported in a train to one of their subordinate camps called Arbeitslager Melk am Donau, better known as Melk.

I knew I was lucky I didn't lose my boots when arriving at Mauthausen, and I had a feeling I wouldn't be so lucky again in the next camp. If some guard liked my boots, they would take them away and make me wear the wooden shoes everyone had to wear, which were very uncomfortable and hard and painful to walk in. So right before we got to Melk, where we were going to get inspected one by one, I asked one of my friends if we could switch only one shoe with one another. He also had a decent pair of shoes so he looked at me intrigued and I explained that nobody would want or care if we only had one good shoe with no match, they would probably let us keep our mismatched pair of decent shoes and once we passed the inspection we could switch back. He liked the idea and agreed.

Our strategy worked perfectly as planned: he was able to keep his good shoes and I was able to keep my good boots until I got back to Prague, after liberation. Much later when they were too tight on me, I was able to exchange them for food.

In Melk, they used to manufacture military products. Almost all the Birkenau boys were considered kids and were sent to work at the "potato house" cleaning and peeling potatoes. Since I was an *Ex-Laufer* from Auschwitz and I was trained and knew what to do, I was assigned as the messenger and barracks assistant to help with cleaning and the distribution of the food.

Everyone else worked outside the camp, and they would commute every day to the factory in three shifts, two during the day and one at night. The last one was the worst since the people came back at sunset but weren't able to sleep since they also had to participate in the daily chores and camp activities.

In some camps, kids had it a little easier than adults, but in others, they were sent directly to the gas chambers. Luckily my age and height let me pretend I was a kid or an adult depending on the circumstances. So, on different occasions, I had to judge what was more convenient for me and stretch as much as I could to look bigger or shrink and act like a kid. If I had made a mistake making these decisions, I wouldn't have survived.

Everyone was complaining about the metal bracelets, they were so tight they cut skin and affected blood circulation in many prisoners. I was able to ask an inmate to duplicate my plaque in aluminum over a piece of leather, so it was much more comfortable and less harmful. I still have that bracelet.

MY LEATHER BRACELET FROM MAUTHAUSEN

Time passed and in April of 1945, the Russian army was once again getting too close to us, so we got orders to board a train and were sent back to the main camp, Mauthausen. We stayed in the main camp for only two days and from there we were sent to a part of Mauthausen called Zeltlager. In this sector there were only Jews and there weren't any barracks, they only had a big circus-like tent. It didn't even have floors, so we had to sleep on the mostly muddy ground without blankets. Food was almost nonexistent. We were lucky if we found potato skins laying around to eat raw. We didn't even get water to drink. It was horrible.

After spending six awful days in that sector, thankfully we were deported in our second and last dead march heading west to Gunskirchen, near Wells. We were all in pretty bad shape, super hungry and thirsty.

When walking through a village in Austria we saw a water well operated by a manual pump. When we tried to get close and get some water, some of the villagers stopped us. I will never forget that act of cruelty. But later we saw next to the road pavement a spinach harvest well packed and organized ready to be loaded in trucks and no one watching it. When walking by it, each of us grabbed a handful of leaves and put them inside our clothes. After the entire convoy went by, there wasn't any spinach left. This march lasted forty kilometers and took three days. I don't remember where or how we slept.

Gunzkirchen was a concentration camp located in the middle of the woods. It was mostly for Hungarian Jews. It had very small, dark, and wet wooden barracks. We had to fit one hundred people in an area less than ten by ten feet so when we first came into the barracks in the afternoon we had to stay standing up, then little by little everyone would accommodate until we were able to find a space to sit down. That's how we slept all night. At night it was pitch black. In spite of it always being rainy, we never had enough drinking or clean water. All the remaining Birkenau boys were there together, which helped us survive. I think we were there for a week, a long dreadful week.

One night I got separated from all my friends, I stayed like five feet away from them. A prisoner from Greece sat down behind me and asked me in the middle of the night to stand up for a minute so he could reposition himself (this was very common) so I did, and when I tried to sit back down, he told me, "I'm sorry, there is no more space for you here."

After standing up for a while I just decided to sit on top of his feet, but he asked me to get up and I did; thinking he would move and make some room for me, but he didn't so I just sat on top of him and didn't get up again. Immediately after, he bit my back and wouldn't let go, so I grabbed my metallic eating tray and started hitting him on the head until he let go. Of course, everyone around us was against me and wanted me to leave so they would get extra space for themselves. I didn't have another option, so I decided to leave the "enemy" territory and walk on top of people towards my friends until I found them. They squeezed together to make room for me, and I was able to sit again. After an hour, the density of the place got back to normal, and we were able to sleep a little.

Other nights, we slept outside in the middle of the woods. Even if it was raining it was better than the dark, wet, and very uncomfortable barrack.

All the prisoners at this camp, including us, contracted lice. And it was probably at that camp where we also contracted *Typhus*. I didn't think we were going to last one more day at that camp.

One morning, in the beginning of May 1945, we saw a small American plane slowly flying over our camp and taking pictures. After that, we heard shotgun shots and then pure silence. At around ten in the morning, we saw the closest German guard leave his station at the camp fence and go to the next guard, he told him something and then they both ran to the next guard, and these three ran to the next one, and so on. They were all getting together and leaving their posts. And just like that, they all left.

X

DORIT: The cruel reality

In Terezin, they would cremate dead people. In the beginning they would put the ashes in a little box with the name of each person and store them. Later on, when the allies were getting closer, they decided to throw away all these boxes in the river that crossed the camp. They asked a group of little children (which included me) to form a human chain and pass the boxes from hand to hand from the storage place to the water. We all thought it was like a game, it was fun, so we started reading the names on the boxes and screaming:

Here goes Mr. Mandelman!

There goes Mrs. Krauss!

Another time, we were playing "ring around the Rosie" at the patio and suddenly a woman jumped from the third floor of the building next to us. She laid on the floor bleeding, all broken up, and we just took two steps to the other side and kept playing. It wasn't all that impressive for us, since we were used to watching all those dead people piled on top of wagons, the same wagons that carried our bread, and paper. Many times, you could hear the peculiar sound of broken arms and legs hanging from the wagon, moving back and forth when being transported. We made up a song using the rhythm of that sound.

There are many things I don't remember about that time. I knew I had to take care of myself, my mom told me what to do and I had to do it all by myself. One day, I got lost and the guards asked me where I was sleeping but I couldn't remember the name of the barrack. Then they asked me when I arrive at the camp, and I said six years ago (which was impossible of course). For me, time and dates didn't exist. Finally, they found my inmate number and were able to take me back to my barrack.

To be honest, I don't know why they let us stay at Terezin all that time. People were usually there temporarily just to be organized and then sent to other concentration camps. My dad was once in a train headed to Auschwitz but at the last minute, they took him out because they needed him to do some electric work. So maybe my dad was really good and needed it at the camp or they forgot about us, or it was just by pure luck, but we managed to all stay together there.

At the beginning, no one knew exactly what was going on at Auschwitz or the other camps, but little by little we started getting some information. Some people would get letters from friends or family members with subtle hints and clues like signing "Take care, Uncle GAS". People were a little confused, I remember everyone discussing what it meant. Also, there were a few people that escaped other camps and came back to tell us what was going on.

There was also a time when the Germans organized a visit from the Red Cross to Terezin, to show them how their "concentration camps" worked and how good the conditions were for their prisoners. Preparing for this, they wanted to do a general cleaning of the place. We had to scrub the walkways, sweep the streets, clean walls, they made nice signs with illustrations for every street, and they even built a glass building with toys in the yard. They put swings and a small carousel but it was only to be used when the Red Cross came.

It was all a show, the day of the visit they gave us a can of sardines that we had to pretend to eat outside; we were instructed to go with it to the German guard and say:

"Uncle Rahm, why are we getting sardines again?!"

As if it was something that happened all the time. They prepared concerts and shows all day, all to impress and camouflage what was really going on. After the Red Cross left the camp, we had to return the sardine cans, they demolished the new building and took all the toys away. Nothing was left.

A few weeks later, they asked people if they wanted to go on a train to Switzerland. Everybody was talking about it, contemplating the idea, thinking if they should go or not, evaluating the risks or possible benefits. But my dad always thought it was a trap. He told us:

"Never say you want to voluntarily go anywhere."

The train left with some people. They in fact arrived in Switzerland and sent letters saying how much better they were and inviting us to go too. A few days later a second train was leaving for Switzerland and everybody wanted to go on it. My dad again said we weren't going anywhere, and it was his final decision. About five thousand people got on the train but this time, they all went straight to the gas chambers.

At some point, I was recruited at the Terezin Theater. My job was to hold on to the different act signs for the plays. I also participated in a play for the German soldiers about flowers. All the girls had paper dresses simulating different flower types and colors. I was Violet. The show was on top of the camp fence, so they had to build a stage for it. We had to sing a song about how soon spring would come, and all the flowers of the camp would bloom and we would enjoy a paradise in freedom. I used to dream about that, and every time we sang the song I cried.

After this play, at the beginning of 1944, we also made a show called *Brundibar*. I was one of the kids singing in the chorus. I was eight years old. They built beautiful drapes made out of rows of flowers that would move so nicely with the wind. The show narrated the story of *Brundibar*, a very bad guy that mistreated the kids. He would make them work hard for him without much pay or food until the kids got together and made a plan to get rid of him, finally they killed him, and all the kids were able to go back to their homes, safe and happy. *Brundibar* wasn't a totally fictitious character. Everybody knew he was inspired by Hitler.

Towards the end of the war, when the allies were getting closer and other camps were being closed, they sent some "lucky" people back to Terezin. They were all sick, weak, hungry, and full of lice. We knew that the camp didn't have much food or space for them either.

Contrary to what anyone would think, if the stronger people got typhus (a lice transmitted disease) they would suffer more potent symptoms than weaker people; in some cases it would be so bad that they would die in just two days. Some of the Typhus infected people weren't even allowed to get off the train. They were so hungry that they would fight and scratch others for a piece of bread. My dad was very scared, he told me not to get too close to them. He managed to find some powder that was supposed to protect us from getting infected, even if we already had lice.

XI

HARRY: My liberation

We didn't know exactly what was going on, but we could feel that the Americans were close. There were two possibilities: either the Germans ran away for good, or they were getting together to fight against the Americans. In this last case, we would still be under German governance and couldn't go anywhere.

The day passed, and we didn't get any food or orders. We didn't know what to do, so we made a war council and voted to keep waiting some more time because it was the safest option. Some prisoners decided to leave and raid the food deposits. We heard there were so many desperate people that it became a very dangerous scene. All my group of friends were patient and smart, so we decided not to go, all but one, and he got hurt.

The next day we realized we couldn't wait there any longer without food or water, so we decided to leave the camp in this wooded area to see what we could find. We saw the dirt road we used to get to the camp a week before and started following it. After walking for half an hour, we could see what looked like a main road. And on it, directing the traffic, there was an American soldier.

Wow! What a surprise, for both of us. He had no idea there was a concentration camp inside those woods. Today there is a monument at that same spot, where the roads meet, recognizing that during the last three months of the war the Nazis created this little concentration camp dependent on the ML Mauthausen, where many people died.

Suddenly, a motorcycle came by with two German soldiers. The American stopped them with a hand gesture. We started yelling and insulting them as bad as we possibly could. The American asked for their guns and one of the Germans, an officer, said he would only surrender to another officer. In a matter of seconds, just like you see in the movies, the American took his gun from his hand and tossed it toward us. He then told them to keep going straight, they could surrender to an officer ahead.

We asked the American what we should do, and he told us to keep walking on that road towards the city of Gunskirchen, where there was a train station and there we could find a big food deposit. We hadn't eaten anything in two days.

We started walking in the direction he pointed us, and we eventually found the deposit. They had sugar, canned meat, and pastas but it was being violently raided. We saw people grabbing food and taking it on wheelbarrows. People were coming from as far as Vienna. We managed to get to the food and got our portions and everyone started making fires outside to cook the food the best they could. For us, it was a feast and we really enjoyed it.

We were there for about three or four days, eating everything we wanted to eat. But a couple of days later we thought it didn't make sense for us to stay there forever so we decided as a group to leave. We grabbed all the food we could carry ourselves and started walking north, towards Czechoslovakia, towards home.

While on the road, a French military truck offered to give us a ride to the town they were headed to. It had a military airport with , and they would probably help us with our repatriation. We accepted their offer and got into the truck that took us to Horsching, near Wels-Austria. Once there, they put us all together in one of the military barracks, but I started to feel a very bad ear pain, so I decided to go by myself to the nearest hospital to be checked by a doctor.

In the hospital, an American military doctor examined me. He took my temperature, which by the way, was the first time in my life I had to put the thermometer in my mouth and not under my arm (the European way), so it seemed a little weird to me. They told me I had a temperature over one hundred and three degrees, which was also weird for me to hear since we were used to hearing temperature measured in centigrade degrees and didn't know what those Fahrenheit degrees meant.

He didn't tell me what was wrong with me, but he gave the nurses instructions to give me a bath, disinfect me, take all the lice, and then check me in a room. They covered me with a white powder (today I know it was DDT pesticide for the lice), then gave me a set of white pajamas. In the hallway, on the way to the room, I ran into one of my Birkenau buddies, Pablo Kummermann. They put us together in a room with four bunk beds, each one slept two people so there was room for eight patients.

After two days at the hospital, I still had the ear pain, and no one was doing anything about it, so I decided it wasn't worth it to stay there and wanted to escape to go back with my friends. I also felt my temperature was still pretty high, so I grabbed a towel and submerged it with cold water and wrapped around my head like a turban and just like that I walked outside through the main doors. The guard gave me a second look, but he let me go.

I went back to the airport with the rest of the group but that night I felt the lice itching again and the pain was getting worse. The following morning, I changed my mind and decided to go back to the hospital. When I got there, I was still conscious enough to realize I couldn't bring in lice with me so I went straight to a bathroom, got rid of the pajamas, took a good shower, and scrubbed as well as I could and went naked to the room I was sharing with Pablo, who was still there. From that day until our return to Prague, we stayed together.

Since I didn't have anything to wear, I grabbed some sheets and a thread I managed to get from the edge of a blanket and made myself some "shorts". These shorts I kept until my return to Prague, and even until I got married. Nobody had told us at the hospital what illness we had, and I never asked either. Until the day they let us go, when one of the nurses told us:

"People that suffered from Typhus have to be careful and take care of themselves!"

So, we finally knew what we had. After three weeks at the Horsching hospital, my fever was gone, and I was feeling much better. They handed us a questionnaire asking us:

"Do you want to return home?"

Both Kummermann and I said yes, and that same day we got new clothes including pants, a shirt, a jacket, shoes, and a blanket that I still have. They took us in a truck to the airport, to the same barracks I was in before. The Birkenau boys were still there, in a Barrack nearby. They told us they don't do anything all day, so they were really bored. They give you food every day, then you go beg the Americans around the compound for chocolate and soap. They were just waiting to be sent back home.

Pablo and I didn't like hearing about that passive waiting. So, after two days we decided to go home on our own, starting the following morning. We told the rest of the boys that we were leaving and if we didn't come back in twenty-four hours, they could assume we weren't coming back to Horsching at all, so they could get our daily meal portions and share it however they wanted.

On June 2nd, 1945, we escaped. We went to the nearest train station and boarded the next train towards Linz. We didn't have any documentation or money, but somehow, we managed to get in. Once we were in the train nobody dared to ask us any questions or ask for tickets. Because of how we looked, they probably knew our story and stayed quiet. When we got to Linz, we looked for the Czech office and found it.

There were people from different countries, and different cities but they knew they couldn't send them all back to Prague at once, especially the ones who weren't Czech, so they had to prioritize and asked us a quick question to know if we were Prague residents:

"What can you find on the San Venceslao Plaza?"

We answered:

"The statue of San Venceslao on his horse."

That was enough for them. They promised they would send us to Prague as soon as they found transportation available. The same day they found room on a truck and put us on it. Linz is a border town of Czechoslovakia, so soon after we were crossing the border and that afternoon we made it to Ceské Budejovice, where we found our friend Johnny Freund, another Birkenau Boy, who forty-five years later still remembers that meeting.

We took a train from Ceské towards Prague. Some good samaritans saw us and realized we were coming back from concentration camps and assuming we were always hungry, gave us a piece of bread and sausage. The train drove through the lake region, stopping next to each one of them. It was a beautiful trip; we enjoyed the scenery. On one of the stops, the train engine was disengaged and left; I knew we couldn't go anywhere without it, at least for a while, so I jumped into the lake for a quick bath in my hospital shorts. A few minutes after, I saw the engine coming back so I quickly got back onto the train still all wet.

We made it to Prague the night of June 3rd, 1945. Our entire trip back lasted thirty-six hours, a lot faster than the official repatriation of the other Birkenau Boys through Vienna and Bratislava. It took them over fourteen days. Now I was home and free, but I didn't know what to do next.

XII

DORIT: The end of the war

I was 9 years old. At the beginning of May 1945, my father saw a truck driving on the road adjacent to the camp. It was filled with people that looked like camp prisoners. He asked them:

"Where are you all headed?"

"To Prague! They answered."

My dad asked them for a ride, and they agreed so we climbed on and a few hours later we made it to Prague. The war wasn't over yet, there were soldiers fighting and shooting everywhere.

The first thing we had to do, before deciding where to go, was to ask for the food booklets, the ones they give prisoners and refugees to get some food since we had no money at all. I also had to go from house to house asking for food, but there were many people coming back from camps and war and even in worse conditions than us. Nobody had enough, let alone extra. We went to some acquaintance's house and hid there for a couple of days.

Then we remembered a very nice lady we met while in Terezin, who had given us her address in Prague in case we made it out of the camp and had nowhere to go. So, we went there. Apparently, she made the same offer to a lot of people because her house was full. I'm not sure how my dad managed to do it, but a few days later we were able to move to a hotel room.

Now, at ten years old, I weighed less than forty-two pounds. People looked at me on the streets as if they were looking at a skeleton. I kind of looked like one. I was really hungry. One day there was a Russian Colonel at our hotel dining room and when he saw me, he ordered a waiter to send us some extra food from him.

A couple of weeks later, my parents decided it was time to go back to my hometown Brno. Usually, it takes only three hours by train, but some of the rails were damaged, so it took us thirty-six hours instead. We were traveling in the animal wagons with open roofs, and sometimes when passing through little towns the people would throw food inside knowing we were coming back from camps. Many times, my parents had to take some food from me to keep me from eating it, if I had eaten all of it, I would have gotten dysentery.

When we finally got to Brno, we had to go to an office to register and say where our home was before the war. Then they would investigate if that information was true and if the house/apartment was empty or who had moved in since we left. If it was a German who was occupying the home, he either ran away already or would be kicked out immediately. But if it was a Czech family, it was harder to vacate.

Luckily our apartment had been occupied by Germans, so we were able to return to it quickly. We slowly started getting our things back, the ones friends and neighbors kept safe for us, even things we simply forgot about or left behind. But a few things we didn't get, and we were told the Russians took them.

I only stayed in Brno for a few days, then my parents decided to send me to my aunt's house in my dad's hometown of Ivancice, so she could watch over me and feed me while my parents went back and forth between Brno and Prague arranging all our paperwork and deciding what to do next. My aunt took me to school, but it didn't last long (classes were done in July) plus I didn't know how to read or write so I was really behind.

After much thought, my parents decided they didn't want to stay anywhere in Europe, so they thought our best option was to go to the United States of America. We filled out and submitted the papers to emigrate. That summer, I went back to Brno and went to see a doctor who after checking my blood values and measurements, put me on all kinds of treatments that lasted a year and a half.

After taking care of my health issues, my parents also worried about me being academically behind compared to the other kids my age, because of all the time I lost being in the camp. So, they managed to get me a private tutor and kept me very busy, always teaching me and enrolling me in as many classes and activities as I had time for, singing, dancing, swimming in the summer, and skiing in the winter.

With Fall came the first day of school. They made me sit on a chair in a corner away from other kids, they knew I recently came back from concentration camps and worried I might still be sick or infected and didn't want the other kids to possibly get what I had. Two weeks later, they called my parents to pick me up because supposedly I had given lice to another girl.

We knew this couldn't be true because the first thing my mom did when we came back home from Terezin was a very thorough disinfection process and she kept checking to make sure I didn't have anything left. So, my mom called the school and asked a doctor to check all the girls in my class, including me! They realized half the class had lice, and I didn't. So, my mom grabbed my hand and told the teacher:

"Now I will take my daughter home because I don't want her to get infected."

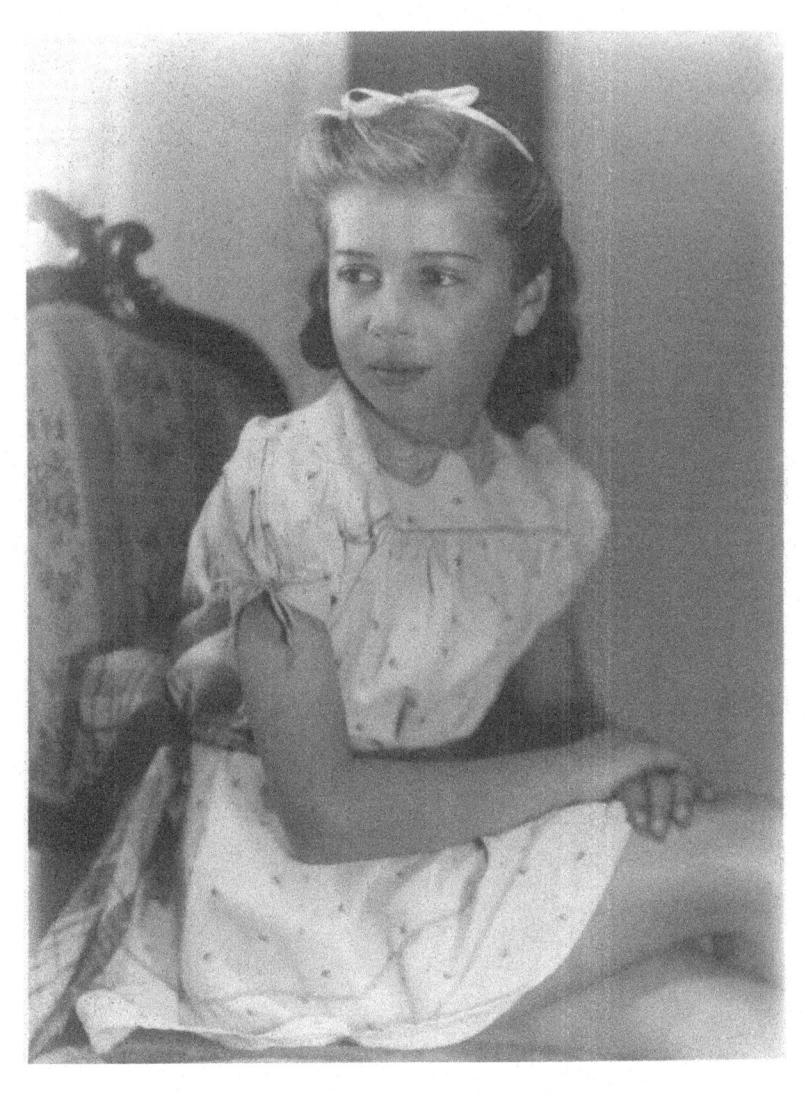

DORIT 12 YEARS OLD

1947

XIII

HARRY: Back to Prague and beyond

I had just turned 16 years old. I started looking for any surviving family members, but I couldn't find anyone right away. I went to a Jewish hospital located in the old neighborhood of Prague. When a nurse saw me, she asked me questions while pointing at different parts of my body:

Does it hurt here? To which I replied, "NO"

Does it hurt here? "NO"

Does it hurt here? "NO"

Does it hurt here? "NO"

Then she told me: - "If nothing hurts you, we can't admit you, do you understand?"

So, then we started again…

Does it hurt here? To which I replied, "yes"

Does it hurt there? "yes"

She helped me get registered and I stayed at the hospital for approximately fifteen days. Then I decided I wanted to make a visit to my dear schoolteacher Karel Vesely. He let me stay in his house for a few days. One day I got a letter from my mom and sister, sent after their liberation, letting me know that they were alive in Bergen Belsen and asking for me and my dad. I wrote back to the Czech officer in charge of repatriation at Bergen Belsen, asking to please send my mom and sister back to Prague as soon as possible since I got back from Auschwitz on my own and needed them.

They wrote back a few days after, telling me where I should go to get help, and food (all of the places I had already visited) and promising they would send my mom as soon as they could. I got this letter the morning of July 3rd, 1945 and that same afternoon my mom and sister arrived in a truck. I took them to the same hospital I went to before and told them to answer that everything hurt so they could get admitted for a few days.

Sometime after, we got an apartment with some furniture. One day while walking around the neighborhood, we ran into the mother of the "Half Jewish" kid from my class; she told my mom, I think more sad than mad:

"It's not fair you see; your full Jewish kids came back and my only half Jewish one didn't!"

My mom was a little shocked to hear that, so she stayed silent for a while. Then she just said:

"I'm so sorry to hear that."

I almost felt guilty at that moment. Why was I able to survive and come back and so many others didn't?

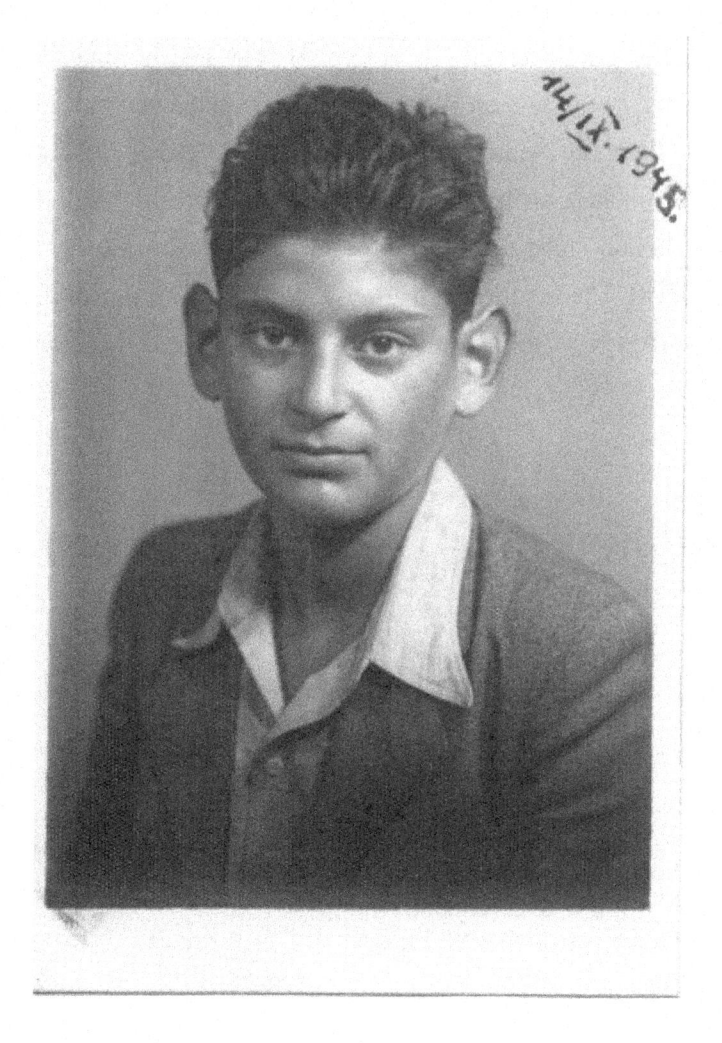

HARRY 16 YEARS OLD

SEPTEMBER 14TH, 1945

We stayed in Prague from 1945 to 1949. I applied to the technical middle school of La Guardia, at Strossmayerovo Námestí, and got accepted. I remember they had us lined up in height order from shortest to tallest and I was the second one in my class. Between September 1945 and July 1946, I grew more than seven inches, so by the end of the school year I stood out from the lineup since my place should have been the sixth now. In June 1949, I passed the test to enter high school and finished the entire five years in just one.

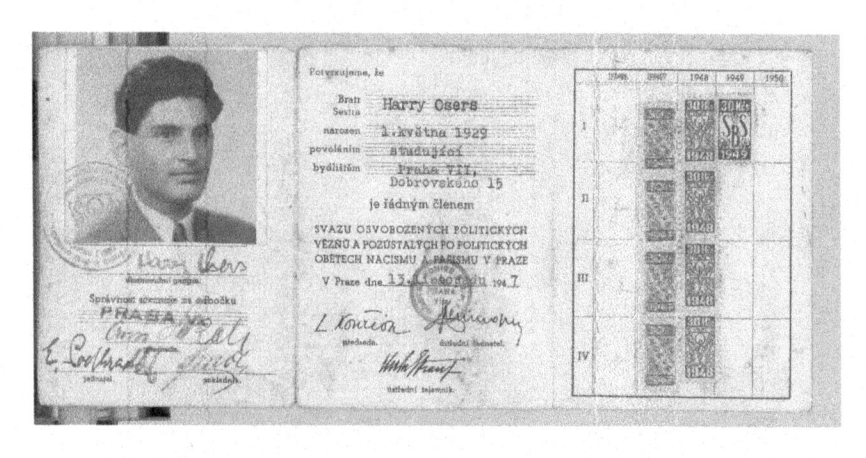

DOCUMENT ISSUED FROM PRAGUE BY THE ASSOCIATION OF POLITICAL PRISONERS DURING THE NAZI REGIME.

13TH NOVEMBER 1947

My sister Sonia met her boyfriend and in 1946 they got married in Prague, but the situation with the Russian communists was getting worse so they were making plans to leave Czechoslovakia and emigrate to another country where they could have a fresh start. Two years later, in 1948, they found a country that was giving immigrant visas to Czech citizens, so they applied and quickly moved across the Atlantic Ocean to Venezuela. Thanks to them, a year later, my mom and I also got Venezuelan immigrant visas. We got them the same day as my high school diploma.

We packed important valuables, and whatever else we could fit in our bags and left our dearest Prague. I remember I saw a postcard from Venezuela that showed a Mountain (Pico Bolívar in Merida, the tallest one in the country) with a little snow at the top. It looked like mountains I've seen around here so I thought maybe that country, that I have never heard of, could be similar to what we have here in Europe.

VENEZUELAN CUSTOMS DECLARATION. 1949

AMERICA VESPUCCI BOAT

We arrived at La Guaira pier in October of 1949. Aside from the tropical hot and humid weather, my first surprise was seeing the guards holding machetes. People were shouting to us in Spanish, (which of course we didn't speak or understand)

"Necesitan ayuda? Meaning "Do you need help?"

But all I could hear was A-Jude-a, and immediately thought they were screaming at us for being Jews, so I wasn't very happy with that welcome.

We finally made it to Caracas, the capital city where my sister was waiting for us. There was a tiny community of Czech immigrants and they all tried to help each other get situated.

I was able to pass my high school equivalency tests because a friend of my mother bought me a Venezuelan history book on Simon Bolivar (the most important military and political leader of Venezuela and Latin America) in Czech and a Czech-Spanish dictionary. He told me to read and study it and I would be fine, especially if I was good at math.

During the oral test, they asked me about Simon Bolivar and when I said, "Simon Bolivar liked the ladies," they told me to stop talking and gave me a passing grade. Then I had to take a test, in Spanish, to get admitted to the university. I passed the test and registered to study civil engineering in the *Universidad Central de Venezuela* (UCV), one of the biggest, and most important universities in Venezuela.

I graduated with honors in March of 1955, and a month later I got married to a Czech girl who also emigrated after the war... Dorit Weiss.

HARRY'S GRADUATION 1955

XIV

DORIT: More changes

One Sunday a group of communist representatives came to our house and left us a form so my dad could register to their political party. One of the questions on the form was religion. My dad didn't like where this was going so he denied it. A couple of days later, my father met with his lawyer, and he told him that if we didn't leave the country soon, we would be in trouble.

So my dad asked around and managed to buy fake Cuban Visas for all of us. With that, we were able to get emigration permits to leave the country. They gave us a list of what we could take with us and they even sent government officers to check we were packing only what was permitted.

My mom offered them coffee in the kitchen so they would get distracted and told me to quickly hide some of our valuables in our bags. We closed the apartment and left everything else inside, we didn't tell anyone we were leaving.

Since we didn't have real visas to go anywhere, we went to France. We lived in France for about six months. My dad was able to find a job in a jewelry store and my mom in a sweater factory. I started going to school. We lived in a hotel room that housed many other immigrants.

One day, my father overheard some people talking about a Latin American country named Venezuela that was giving away immigrant visas. So he called the embassy and asked for an appointment. We went there, asked for our visas, and they asked us to do a few health tests. When my mom had her blood pressure measured, they told her it was too high and they wouldn't give her a visa because Caracas, Venezuela's capital, is too elevated and it would be bad for her health to go there.

She told us to get our visas and go; that she would stay in France or go back to Prague until we could find a place where we can all be together. But my dad immediately said we would do it together, so he asked the consulate if they could take her blood pressure in a couple of weeks to see if it was any better, they agreed. The second time around, my mom's pressure was normal, and we all got our visas.

My parents wanted to fly to Venezuela, but for some reason I wanted to travel by boat. I insisted so much that I convinced them to do it my way. Since the boat tickets were much cheaper than the plane ones, we used the extra money to take a mini vacation to the French Riviera before our trip.

We arrived in Caracas on January 19th, 1949. And we heard the news that the plane my parents wanted to take to come here crashed in the Azores Islands. When we disembarked at the La Guaira pier, my dad saw someone holding a banner with his name on it. He was confused because he wasn't expecting anyone since he didn't know anybody in Venezuela. When we got closer, he realized the person holding the banner was Mr. Klein, a family friend, who heard we were coming and was waiting for us. He had left Czechoslovakia before the war to go to Shanghai and then came to Venezuela.

After explaining everything he took us to his home. We stayed with his family for a month until my dad found us an apartment.

I started studying in the American School; there you could choose classes in Spanish or English but there were many kids that spoke other languages. I couldn't speak or understand any Spanish or English, so school was really hard for me, and my parents couldn't help me either.

DORIT 15 YEARS OLD (1949-1950)

ESCUELA AMERICANA

My mom found a job as the treasurer of a popular Viennese bakery shop and since she always got home late from work, I had to cook dinner for the three of us. I wasn't really good at it. In the beginning I was burning everything. I was seventeen years old then.

When I graduated from high school, I knew I didn't want to go to college for a long academic bachelor's degree, so instead I decided to go to a technical commercial academy. I received a two-year administration degree and then went to work as an accountant.

In October of 1949, I met Harry Osers, a Czech boy that had just arrived from Prague the day before. For me it was love at first sight, but he probably didn't notice me until a year later. We dated for five years and got married on April 16th, 1955.

OUR WEDDING DAY

XV

HARRY: Together in Venezuela

In the following years, I became a professor of engineering and architecture at the University (UCV) and published several textbooks on civil and structural engineering that are still being used internationally today.

Dorit and I understood each other. Coming from the same background and having a lot in common, we were able to help each other heal and enjoy our life. Venezuela offered us a second opportunity to start our lives, and we took it. We adapted to its people, their culture, their weather, but always keeping our roots and traditions alive. We traveled around the country visiting beautiful places like the Caribbean coast beaches, Merida State Mountains, and pretty lakes. We celebrated Jewish Holidays at home. We spoke Czech at home and Spanish to our grandkids. We cooked our traditional Czech food but also enjoyed Venezuelan cuisine. We were really happy.

We even went back to visit Terezin and Auschwitz. I also reunited with some of the survivors from the Birkenau Boys. I have spoken and given lectures in several Holocaust remembrance acts.

Venezuela was also the birthplace of our three sons Rodolfo, Tomas, and Miguel; all of whom became successful engineers and professors. They gave us five grandchildren, and eight great-grandchildren (so far). It was finally in our home in Venezuela where Dorit was able to have her own flower garden.

This is to me my most precious victory, and a huge achievement over the Nazis. They could have destroyed me like a bug, but they didn't, and instead we reproduced and formed a new and even bigger Jewish-Venezuelan family.

Epilogue

This is the story of my grandparents. I'm only one of the five grandchildren of the brave and courageous main characters of this story. I'm a Social Communications major, a journalist, my responsibility is to communicate their atrocious story in the best possible way. My only suffering was to know everything they had to go through in their lives and thinking the rest of the world might never know about it because they don't have the opportunity to meet them, talk to them, or read it somewhere. It's not ok that so many people ignore what happened and even go so far as to deny it.

Even if the few holocaust survivors live many more years and are willing to tell their stories, time passes and in a few years, there will be none of them left. After that, we (the children and grandchildren of survivors) will not be in this world either. So, this is the only way to keep these memories and stories alive, so that they can transcend decades and generations and never be forgotten.

My grandfather was a professor and my grandmother a storyteller by nature. So thankfully they were both always willing to teach us, and tell us what they could remember, and transmit all of their knowledge about the war not only to us, family, and friends, but to everyone who wanted to know and hear about it. I feel lucky that not only could I listen to their experiences directly from them, (on many occasions) and ask them questions, but I could also learn so much from them.

For example, in my grandparents' house, you were never allowed to throw away food; you had to ask for only what you knew you would eat and finish all of the food you were served so no food was wasted. They said after being hungry so many days of their lives they couldn't allow food to go to waste. Also, before throwing away any electronics, my grandfather would take apart the working pieces in case he could reuse them later to fix another one.

My grandmother spoke five fluid languages: Her native Czech, she had to learn German during the war, French when she lived in France, Spanish when she moved to Venezuela and English. She taught me how important and useful this was. Today I can speak Spanish, English, some French and some Hebrew.

Now it is my turn to share what I know with people that didn't have the same opportunity as me. It's my duty to remember and spread their words. They deserve that.

Eventually I want my kids to read this book and also learn about their great grandparent's story, how brave, and smart they were and how hard they had it in life, but because of their strength and perseverance they survived and succeeded. Because of that, we are here.

Before writing this book, I did a little research of my own, watching holocaust movies and reading other survivors' stories. Soon I realized my grandparent's story was a special contribution to the material that was out there. All these stories are. I quickly began to gather all the material I had from them, including photos, interviews, videos, and manuscripts and started writing.

In the book, *Made to Stick,* from the authors Chip Heath and Dan Heath, I once read a theory they call "The curse of knowledge." According to this, when a person knows a lot about a specific subject, they assume their audience knows the same as they do, and they tend to skip details or leave out explanations. I tried my best to write this book in the most detailed and descriptive way, but without modifying or altering their story. I have probably failed at some point and surrender to the curse, and if so, I'm sorry.

My goal was to write a short, easy to read book that recounted the story of both my grandparents in a way that anybody could read it; starting with my friends and family, then complete strangers, from seniors to teenagers, from busy businesspeople to stay at home parents, and maybe even Oprah one day. And of course, my most important readers were my grandparents.

The first edition I wrote in my native language, Spanish, and my family self-published a few copies of the book in our country, Venezuela. Unfortunately, my grandmother passed away before the book was printed, but at least she knew about its existence. My Grandfather passed away in 2013, he was able to read the printed book.

I decided to do the second edition, in English, when my first two daughters, Nicole and Aileen, were old enough to go to elementary school and before we had our third daughter. Not only to please many English-speaking friends that have been asking and patiently waiting to read it, but also to be able to reach a bigger audience and once more share this story as much as I can.

Thank you for letting me do that.

Angie

Acknowledgment

A special thank you...

To my younger sister Judith Osers for doing all the graphic design and book formatting.

She likes when I say she is the youngest!

To my husband Abe Sultan for always pushing me to do my best; and for supporting me in every possible way. Love you!

And lastly, to my "book club friends" for encouraging me to write this book in English -my second language- and for your kind praise words.